# What Others Are Saying

*"Unlimited - Anything is Possible" is a new book by Glen Klassen which brings an even greater depth of understanding to his first wonderful book, "Evansing". Written in a friendly, flowing and easy to understand narrative, the book draws on the experiences in a story about love, learning, and growing up to illustrate the more profound lessons about purpose, passion, wisdom, gratitude and hope. You will find yourself effortlessly gaining an understanding of how to find your passion and move forward in your own life. Guaranteed, you will feel that you are "Unlimited" and that "Anything is Possible"!*

**Cecilia Grinham**, CFO and Business Development Manager, Entrepreneur, Coach and Facilitator

*I recommend wholeheartedly, this book-"Unlimited - Anything is Possible." Glen Klassen is able to inter weave each quality of having a successful life in sensitive, engaging, thought provoking ways that make sense & inspire me to become someone greater than I am today. Glen combines values, quotes & Evansing illustrations in a seamless flowing narrative. The theme of empowerment inter-sects with: awareness; courage; mentorship; doing the hard things; purpose; passion; removing obstacles; wisdom; gratitude & hope making Glen's book rich with insight; interactive with my heart, mind & emotions & a great read.*

**Arnie Chamberlain**, Chaplain, Carewest

*In his second and latest book "Unlimited - Anything is Possible", author Glen Klassen builds on his novel "Evansing - Heart of the Irish Kingdom" in a clever and creative manner. Combining his personal coaching background and interest in proactively managing change, he uses the main character "Edwin" as an example to portray and define the key principles of taking* charge of our lives. "Unlimited - Anything is Possible" is an interesting and inspiring statement on reaching your potential and will make you want to read "Evansing - Heart of the Irish Kingdom!"

**Brian Lukyn**, Author of "The Un-Retirement GuideTM : A Complete Life Wellness PlanTM for 50+ Boomers Needing to Succeed!"

"Unlimited – Anything is Possible" is a sensible and matter of fact approach to raising one's sights and one's lot in life. To lift our fortunes, we need to take definite and determined actions through evaluating our circumstances (awareness) and exercising our options. Hope is released when we act. Hope helps us to be willing to over-come our fears and limitations. As we raise our expectations, we are encouraged and feel gratification and excitement. We need to hear more of this! Encouragement to think 'Unlimited' is so important and needed today.

**Harley Torgerson**, CEO, Hatco Projects Inc.

*Glen's new book, "Unlimited — Anything is Possible," is an eye opener. A true breath of fresh air, it is an enlightening and easy to read book, that is truly helpful. While reading, you get the feeling that you are having a discussion over coffee with Glen. The information is delivered with ease, and is so inspiring, that you won't want to stop reading. It is rare that I finish a book, and want to thank the Author, yet I find myself doing just that. Thanks Glen!*

**Mike Gilhooly**, President, Jo-Co Interiors Ltd.

*"Unlimited — Anything is Possible" invites you to re-write your own history and knock down barriers that keep you from living your best life. I recommend this book to the individual who wants to meet and exceed their own potential. Glen gives them practical tools, and encourages the honest self-reflection that can make it a reality."*

**Colette Murray RDH**, Access Dental Hygiene Services

*I found Glen's new book, "Unlimited - Anything is Possible" inspiring and really having me want to be a better person.... better at what we do and who we are to both ourselves and others. It presents life lessons through very thought provoking situations without being cliché. I was impressed and truly moved to take a real look at myself in the mirror and want to be better.*

**Greg Travnicek**, Marketing and Web Development Expert

*Glen Klassen's book, "Unlimited – Anything is Possible" IS a valuable tool for anyone looking to accomplish something more in their life. A quick easy read packed with the tools you need to succeed in life. Glen kept me engaged by sprinkling colorful illustrations and real life examples and anecdotes throughout this book. Well done, Glen!*

**Russ Dantu**, Professional Speaker

*Glen's new book, "Unlimited - Anything is Possible" is a thought-provoking book and will challenge any reader to new possibilities. Anyone can become more than they are today and this book will allow you to coach yourself to higher levels. Glen's insights and discoveries reflect his desire to grow and see growth in others. Anything is possible.*

**Linda Olson**, CEO of Christian Speakers Get Paid, Amazon #1 Bestselling Author of "Uncovering the Champion Within"

*Glen Klassen writes like a wizard, he will take you on a wonder ride through his new self-help book based on comparisons to his first book "Evansing — Heart of the Irish Kingdom." I have read a lot of self-help books but Glen's book is gripping and on point. I would put Glen's book on the top of my pile that I recommend good books to friends right beside Dale Carnegie.*

**Trevor Carter**, Owner of D'Angelo Photography

As I have gone through my journey of self-discovery it has called for me to go deeper and deeper. Sometimes you are pleasantly surprised but oft times you are asking, do I want to continue looking further? Glen's new book helps you understand why these blocks seem to pop up and he gives you great techniques to move past the fear. I would strongly recommend you pick up this book and go through it to help you become everything you were born to be.

**Paul Hauk**, CEO, BeneCo Inc.

"For those of us who are seeking a deeper sense of joy and peaceful completion in our lives, UNLIMITED is a helpful and impactful resource. Glen Klassen provides a smooth and practical tool kit in this all in one transformational book. Any person seeking a better life would make this a 'must do' in their daily discipline."

**Kathleen D. Mailer**, International Business Evangelist, #1 Best Selling Author (*Walking In The Wake of the Holy Spirit; Living An Ordinary Life, With an Extraordinary God),*

Founder/Facilitator of "A Book Is Never A Book Boot Camp", Editor-In-Chief of Today's Businesswoman Magazine.

*This book is brilliant. Not only has the author captured the key components of what it takes to be successful but he has skillfully illustrated the principles using excerpts from his novel "Evansing – Heart of the Irish Kingdom." The author will take you on an incredible journey to empower you to get above or stay above the line. As you start to apply these principles anything is possible.*

**Suzanne D Jubb**, Author, The Golden Goose, One Important Step to Financial Success.

# UNLIMITED

## ANYTHING IS POSSIBLE

Glen E. Klassen

# Table Of Contents

# Preface

Life is a mystery. It has all sorts of unexpected twists and turns. Many of these happened outside of our control. They were experiences foisted upon us by others and seemingly chance events. However many of these twists and turns also came as a result of our own choices and actions. The outcome of these choices and actions ultimately form our life. A life of reflecting with satisfaction on how it has turned out, or a life of tormenting regrets.

Many people never realize they do have a choice as to the life they experience. They believe things just happen to them and are beyond their control. Consequently they blame bad breaks, bad people, bad economy etc. In coaching circles this is known as living below the line. The attitude of blaming influences outside of themselves leads to excuses and even denial. The result is a life of feeling helpless and hopeless. The individual who lives below the line has no sense of control over their life experiences. This results in an unhappy life with only a small portion of their potential being realized.

People who live above the line know they are essentially in control of their lives. They recognize there will be events outside of their control. They also recognize by increasing their capacity to participate and be present in life they can increase the odds in their favor. By doing so they put into motion forces that will work to their advantage and even minimize the effects of those seeming unfortunate experiences.

The objective of this book is to empower people to get above the line and if you are already above, to stay above. I wrote the novel, "Evansing – Heart of the Irish Kingdom" (Evansing) which will be used to illustrate the principles necessary for you to coach yourself above the line. As you start to apply these principles you will increasingly know life to be unlimited and that anything is possible.

Happy coaching!

# Awareness- Part One

*Chapter One*

There is a very basic requirement for a successful life. It is awareness. It is mandatory for creating solutions in life that will move us forward. The concept in life of awakening and becoming aware is a very foundational truth. It is essential to growth. Until a person knows there is a better way of doing life, he or she will have no motivation to change or even a capacity to know change is necessary. As well, a person must have at least some basic belief in their ability to achieve the desired change and a willingness to take the necessary steps. The flip side to truths is lies. We all have them, passed down to us generationally, in our family of origin, faulty interpretations of childhood experiences and the molding by an imperfect society. Lies act to impair our ability to identify what is true and know what are necessary changes for a successful aware life. To be willing to admit the possibility that some of our beliefs are lie based can be a very big step and a necessary step in order to start creating awareness. Indeed it may be the first and most important step of awareness.

Familiarity with someone can interfere with our ability to see them with eyes of truth. In other words it can keep us from experienceing new awareness of them changing. They may have done a one hundred and eighty degree change from who they were before, but we may still see them as the misfit we've known them to be. Familiarity with a certain type of situation or problem may also block us in our perception to understand things are no longer the same and require a different approach.

What is awareness? It is a new more accurate way of looking at things we have never considered before. It may be something very mundane that literally shocks us when we realize we have believed a lie. Other times it could be something much more serious. For example a friend who gave me permission to share this, once believed he had contributed to his father's death. This tormented him for a period of time. When he shared this with me I simply told him he had swallowed a lie. He looked kind of surprised and then said, "Yes, you are right I have swallowed a lie." The torment left him.

Of course not all blocks to our awareness are so easily identified and removed. For deeply rooted issues created by painful experiences, especially if in our childhood, can take a prolonged effort to develop the level of awareness we require to live life well. When children suffer scars in their psyche it can leave them with a plethora of influences impairing their awareness. This often stays with them even as they become adults.

The hero in Evansing, Edwin, had suffered such a childhood.

"One morning after a particularly fitful night's sleep and almost non-stop nightmares, Edwin decided he needed to do something different. As hard as it was to imagine life being any different or somehow better than now, he determined he had to at least try."

The above excerpt from Evansing illustrates awareness. In this case the awareness is at a minimal level, but it is nevertheless awareness. Edwin had been experiencing a high degree of dissatisfaction which fueled his realization of needing to do something different. This new awareness now made possible the next step.

An essential requirement for becoming a-wake and aware is teachableness. This may result from an external source, such as an expert on some subject or simply an internal stirring. There needs to be a willingness to acknowledge that one's present course or beliefs may be erroneous or at least need an adjustment to ensure a better outcome in some aspect of one's life.

A major block to teachableness is pride. When we believe we know everything and nobody can tell us anything, that is pride. When we are endued with this quality, it can create disaster in our finances, relationships, and even our health. There is an old saying, "Pride goes before a fall." Pride can be a major inhibitor to a person's capacity to recognize that they are in error. A person who never acknowledges a need to learn more is likely experiencing a serious pride issue. In coaching circles, it is called the "I know." When someone's automatic response to a piece of information is "I know," then you have someone who struggles with teachableness. The reality of life is that, no matter what the subject matter, there is always another level of truly knowing and understanding. Or to put it in terms relating to our topic, there is always a greater measure of awareness to be gained.

"The bird was telling him his thoughts of going to the monastery were good and he was to ask for a particular monk called Percival. As Edwin pondered what was going on he started to experience something else he had not felt before. He believed it must be what is known as hope."

Here we have an important result of awareness – hope. I cover the topic of hope later on which includes an expanded version of the excerpt given above. When a person has been released from a limitation that has robbed one of hope, it invariably brings hope. This new hope makes one able to experience even more awareness. This is due to hope's powerful capacity to empower a person to expect good things. This opens a person to believing anything is possible and therefore willing to act in ways not previously even considered.

# Awareness- Part Two

*Chapter Two*

Awareness is of no use if a person does not respond in some concrete way, either to begin something new or to quit doing something contrary to the well-being of self or others. There must be courage to take steps to implement the required change. This can be very difficult, especially if there is a lot of investment tied into the previous belief and behavior. There have been examples of military commanders still going ahead with battle plans even after new intelligence indicated that the plans would not work. Their ego investment would not allow them to change and the results were disastrous with many lives needlessly lost. Of course even everyday opportunities to change can be ignored simply because it's uncomfortable. Quite often this is due to some sort of fear of the consequences of the change, even when it is apparent it will lead to better long-term benefits. People can have fear of failure or even fear of success. This will result in a person staying in a dead end job or abusive relationship because it's familiar and in a perverse way, comfortable.

It is worth investing a little more time on the topic of fear. I once heard in a movie trailer that "fear rots the brain." That is a very succinct and accurate representation of the effects of fear. It distorts our thinking. Fear blocks one's awareness or at least can impair our willingness to acknowledge the new awareness trying to take root in our consciousness. This can be due to the new awareness being costly in some manner. Perhaps it will affect our finances or maybe we need to release a relationship. Whatever the cost it is important to recognize the awareness that has arisen and be willing to not let the fear of loss influence our decision. All true awareness has the purpose of improving our long-term well-being even if there is a sacrifice in the short-term. Of course this raises the question of accurate discernment as to what appears to be a new awareness. In the event of a serious con-sequence it is wise to get counsel from someone we trust or go to an authoritative source able to give us a definitive answer.

Let us be people who are open to the possibility of being wrong in even some of our most cherished beliefs and actions. Let us be people with the courage to take steps to implement necessary changes.

"Edwin gathered his paltry belongings... The Ireland he lived in required its men to be warriors. There was no other way to be a man except for those strange monks and priests which now Edwin was going to visit. The nearest monastery was almost fifteen miles away. He went with a spring in his step and an expectancy of something very different but good awaiting for him there."

Often and perhaps always when awareness sparks new action there will be resistance.

"Up ahead he could see two men standing by the side of the road. They looked menacing."

Edwin overcame that challenge. It occurred in the course of him pursuing a new life sparked by his growing awareness.

To develop greater awareness a person must start asking themselves questions as to why they are choosing to take a particular course of action or choosing to react or respond in a certain way. We often simply choose to do something without appreciating the reason for it. A good habit to develop is to pause and consider the courses of action that are available to us, especially when there is potential for consequences beyond the obvious. The objective is to evaluate the best possible outcome. When we have already made decisions a useful exercise is to review the reasons for our decisions and ask ourselves if a better one could have been made.

Other questions to ask ourselves are of a more personal and internal nature. Questions such as: Why do I think what I think? Why do I do what I do? Why do I believe what I believe? Why do I expect what I expect? Answers to these questions may well lead to deeper questions as to values and unresolved wounds from past experiences. In other words how are those values and unresolved wounds influencing me?

An important thing to keep in mind is to be patient with the process of growing in awareness. A useful exercise is to keep a journal where we write our thoughts about decisions we are considering. We can write down the above questions and their answers. By having these written down we are able to review them and more readily determine patterns about ourselves that will help us understand what makes us tick. For example we may notice how we have made a number of rather impulsive decisions. Then we also note that each time there was a fear fueling that decision. When evaluating the outcome of those decisions we further note that they were always less than satisfactory. This new awareness should give us cause to pause when we feel fear for we know we are now susceptible to a less than ideal decision. Then we need to ask ourselves why we feel afraid and if it is valid or not and how to resolve it.

To encourage our growing awareness it is important to nurture it with gratitude. The act of giving thanks for each new awareness will spark even more awareness and the necessary actions in response to that awareness. This directly leads to a more satisfying life in alignment with our purpose. As we start to envision the new life being birthed in us, it creates the desire necessary to propel us toward the life we know we are intended to live. As we are engaged in being thankful for what we have we are growing in faith for even more blessings coming to us in the future. It activates attraction of the right good things into our life. This in turn empowers us to actively be involved in taking those steps leading to the fulfillment of our life goals.

# Limitless Thinking – Part 1
## *Chapter Three*

Limited thinking decreases our likelihood for true success. In fact it totally eliminates the likelihood of it ever happening. We all have been placed here for something glorious and amazing. It will require us to be stretched beyond our normal capacity and experience. We are meant to live a life without limits.

Of course there are resistances to living a life without limits. They are known as fear and discomfort. Refusing to face our fears and an unwillingness to experience discomfort has limited many people to living predictable lives far short of their potential. I am reminded of seeing Olympic downhill skiers racing down a slope even when the conditions are treacherous. They refuse to play it safe. They have one goal in mind and that is to win the gold medal.

Edwin had such a decision to make. He realized there was a raiding party from an enemy kingdom. He then warned a nearby village of the danger. They started to get ready to defend themselves. When the villagers discovered that the enemy was headed away from them toward another village they disagreed with Edwin as to the next step.

"The chieftain started to talk over with some of the clan's leaders whether it was wise to risk their lives for people down the road. They would be against a party far superior to them in size. Edwin interrupted them and said it was the only right thing to do. He encouraged them to consider that next time it may be their turn to have the people down the road help them. Several of the men told Edwin to mind his own business. The chieftain said his priority was the safety of his village... He did not think it wise to endanger his people when the odds were so against them. Further imploring was useless. Edwin decided he could not stay with them."

Like Edwin, sometimes we will recognize the need to no longer hang out with certain people. Everyone is on their own journey and consequently in different stages of life. When we have a clear sense of wanting to do something heroic so our life makes a difference, there will be a need to be willing to move on, sometimes alone. Winston Churchill demonstrated heroism throughout his life. He volunteered for dangerous military missions as a young man and even into his forties. By the time he was in his late fifties and into his mid-sixties, he was willing to look foolish and be cast aside for his views on the rising danger of Hitler and Germany. Most people ignored him and considered him of no consequence during the time running up to the Second World War. It was a lonely time for Churchill. But he was a man of integrity and did not change the expression of his views to please the masses.

Then one day he was summoned by the King and asked to be the Prime Minister. This appointment led to his fulfilling a very difficult role and firmly established him in history as a great man living without limits.

Alone, Edwin decided to see what he could do on his own about the invading party.

"At first Edwin couldn't hear anything, but after about two hundred yards he started to hear the rearguard of the Tissus party. The raiders were unusually loud, which indicated they must be extremely confident, even to the point of being overconfident. Was it because they had an extra-large number of men or was it because of something else which gave them an advantage?"

Living without limits requires courage. In this case Edwin's courage gave him awareness as to what was unusual about the behavior of the raiders and then be able to evaluate different possible reasons for it. He discovered they had Alwyn, a powerful Druid priest with them and he surmised this gave the raiders their confidence.

"Edwin continued to gain ground and wondered how he could make a difference with such a large force. A thought came to him. He had his bow and a full quiver of arrows. With one arrow he could take out Alwyn and the whole Tissus base of confidence would be gone."

Limitless thinking opened Edwin to receive thoughts that now made possible a situation when only moments before it looked impossible. It reminds me of David facing Goliath. An unarmed teenager except for a slingshot and some stones facing a heavily armed and armored foe. Yet he defeated Goliath in dramatic fashion. He actually ran toward the giant telling him he was going to cut his head off. By the way, David didn't even have a sword. He counted on using Goliath's own sword for that. His limitless thinking resulted in David being catapulted into a whole new life.

Edwin found himself in such a situation:

"With great care and self-assurance Edwin drew back his bow and aimed at Alwyn's heart. Then with deadly accuracy the arrow went straight into Alwyn's heart."

Mission accomplished, but now he needed to get away.

# Limitless Thinking – Part 2
## Chapter Four

Edwin's courage and noble way of being had attracted the attention of some very powerful people. Consequently as he is running for his life he is rescued in a most unexpected way.

Sometimes our lives will experience something almost akin to that because of our determination to refuse to accept limits on what is possible for our lives.

As indicated in the previous chapter, Edwin was also prepared for the opportunity when it came. He had established great skill with his bow and could confidently release the arrow knowing it would hit its mark. The other area of preparation was his development of courage and a noble way of being. It is interesting to note that even though in many ways Edwin had a rough violent way about him, he also had a side of wanting to do the right thing. Sometimes we may be frustrated by a perceived lack of the qualities we think we need in order to achieve some amazing accomplishment. We don't have to be perfect. However we need to know which qualities are especially important for us to focus on and develop. Edwin's desire for something better led him on the path of where to place his focus in his development. It undoubtedly was messy and wouldn't have looked very smooth to an outside observer, but it was accomplishing the necessary changes in Edwin. In order for us to be prepared there needs to be the motivation to do the preparation. This will require us to connect with our passion, genius and calling in life.

The next time you feel you don't have what is necessary to achieve some great aspiration, stop and ask yourself, "Why do I think that way?" Chances are some bruises you've experienced along life's way have shrunk your expectations as to what is poss-ible for you. If you experience fear when considering some great feat then it is necessary to face it. The fear could be broken down in bite size pieces. Say for example you realize pursuing your goal will entail lots of public speaking. You could start facing that fear by taking every advantage to speak up in staff meetings or other public venues. Joining Toastmasters or taking a Dale Carnegie course will give you training in being a public speaker. Or perhaps there are some other skills you need to consider developing or strengthening. Whatever the reason, refuse to accept it as being the last word on whether you can achieve your goal. To put it another way, think about an empty balloon. It requires effort to expand it. You need to blow into it and keep blowing into it until it reaches its desired size. So it is with expanding the limits we have placed on our lives. It requires a determined effort to push out those boundaries. Unlike a balloon our possibilities are unlimited. We just need to keep placing a demand on ourselves to see us expand beyond anything we could have dreamt possible.

Start developing a mindset of "Yes, I can do that" whenever facing a new challenge. Progressively your automatic response of "I can" will replace the old automatic response of "I can't." If necessary seek wise counsel and support concerning your desire to accomplish a shift in your mindset.

Reminders of different types can be useful. My daughter and her husband bought a T-shirt for me which reads "No Limits." When I wear it I feel more inclined to believe I have no limits on me. All things become possible.

In pursuing a life without limits, having a mentor can be a tremendous asset for providing practical insights, valuable contacts and timely encouragement. Check your circle of influence for someone you respect and who you know carry the qualities and proven success you want to gain from. An important attribute for a quality mentor is that they genuinely have your best interest at heart and are able to assess your desires from the perspective of what is right for you. They ensure they are not unduly influenced by the conventional, for going after a life with no limits is not conventional. As well, it is preferable to have someone whose company you enjoy and into whom you can contribute value as well.

To pursue the unlimited lifestyle requires a willingness to live with ambiguity and ob-stacles. The former is by definition unclear and the latter can be disheartening. While on the path to the unlimited you will see clues indicating this is the way, but there will also be signs that seem to indicate you have taken the wrong way. The key thing to keep in mind is that it is an inherent part of the journey and the right response is to realize even the seeming wrong turns are part of the preparation. Therefore progress is being made even when it doesn't appear to be. To get past obstacles, a person must be more inspired by the objective being pursued than discouraged with the obstacles in the way. In other words the level of desire for the attainment of the objective must be high enough to keep one pressing through whatever is in the way.

"High expectations are the key to everything."

Sam Walton, founder of Walmart

High achievers like Sam Walton expect to achieve far over and above what average achievers expect. They dream and dare greatly.

Ponder the power working in you to give you the ability to do even beyond what you can imagine.

# Mentors – Part 1
## *Chapter Five*

In monastic Ireland, St Brigid is credited with the following quote:

"Go off and don't eat until you have found a soul friend, because anyone without a soul friend is like a body without a head. The water of a limey well is not good to drink nor good for wishing. It is like a person without a soul friend."

In Celtic Ireland communities of people would support one another. They would be soul friends to each other. So it could be said that in Irish Celts history the role of mentoring was very important to the sustainability of their oft difficult lives.

Edwin had just entered into a brand new life. While most attractive compared to his old life, it also entailed grave new responsibilities and greater authority by which Edwin could do much good or much evil. He required a mentor to help him with the process of becoming the man he needed to be. That man was Percival, a wise man somewhat more senior than Edwin and a close friend to King Erith. Through Percival's wise counsel, Edwin learned how to read and write, received instruction on forgiveness and healing of his heart, as well as insight on how to be in relationship with Princess Greer.

Everyone should have a mentor in their life. We all have areas of life that are beyond the scope of our ability to handle well without outside counsel. Yes, some of us will do fairly well without a mentor. However, if we are to do *really* well we will need a mentor. That mentorship could be in the form of several friends whose collective wisdom provides you with much needed insight and encouragement. It could be someone who is an expert in your field and you are able to ask them about business or technical issues. Whatever form your mentor or mentors take, it is essential to have at least one. For just like those in Celtic Ireland, life is too tough without one.

Working effectively with a mentor requires certain qualities and ways of being so that the relationship is satisfying for both parties.

Here again we have the attitude of teachableness playing a vital role in the person being mentored. If you are asking someone to invest their time and energy into your life then it would behoove you to be open to doing what they recommend. For example if your mentor recommends you read a book, then one of the very first things for you to do is get that book and start reading. In this way you demonstrate your respect for your mentor. It is a prime way to honor their counsel.

In Evansing an example of how a promising mentoring relationship could look is illustrated as follows:

"Percival was the epitome of grace in the way he related to Edwin. He had a comforting fatherly way about him, which nurtured the soul and spirit of Edwin. It was though Edwin had been waiting for someone like Percival all his life. He was glad he now had the opportunity to connect with someone of the caliber of Percival. Not only did they talk about Edwin, but also Edwin was able to ask Percival about himself and why he became a monk."

Another great indicator is how time flies and the friendship grows:

"Both men were surprised to discover how the time had flown by. In some ways it seemed like they had only spoken for moments and had only touched the surface on a few things. On the other hand they knew they had created new links of friendship, which would benefit them both."

There should be some clear objectives with respect to your mentoring sessions. In Evansing, Edwin had clear objectives:

"Being a truly noble and excellent man became Edwin's number one objective. He also had this driving consuming desire to be an amazing husband for Greer."

Having a mentor who has had depth of life experiences relevant to your objectives is of course paramount. Percival was such a man:

"Percival had been married only briefly, as his wife had died in childbirth with their first child. During his two year marriage he came to greatly cherish his wife. It was that experience and the several months of courting, which helped Percival to input into Edwin what was needed to help with the process of preparing him for Greer. As well, he had twelve years gentling of his personhood and refinement of his faith connection. This gave him a pool to draw upon in order to provide valuable input for Edwin. Of course this was not only for his future marriage with Greer, but also for all the challenges which lay before him."

# Mentors – Part 2

*Chapter Six*

To be effective a mentor must be willing to stand up to you and ensure you do the hard things even when you don't want to. It's not his role to only be your friend and curry your popularity. His role is to be an agent of change for your best. Here we have Edwin initially resisting Percival's plan for him:

"Tonight I think it is most important for you to express to me more about the pain of growing up alone much of the time and being rejected by other members of your community. Let's separate the rejection that came first because of your uncle's reputation and then secondly what came because of your own behavior.'

'How can that get me where I want to go and be? We've talked about it already. Let's talk about new things, important things.'

'Those are very important things. Unless they are resolved and healed it will forever taint your motives and aspirations. You will operate out of a need to prove and approve of yourself instead of knowing you are proved and approved.'

Edwin looked at him a little frustrated and said, 'Okay let's do it your way."

Working with a mentor requires trusting their judgment and that they have your best interest at heart. As well it may require a shift in one's perspective, so as to appreciate those things one finds distasteful are actually leading to a more fulfilling life. This is shown as follows:

"The next morning before Jaffa came to get him up; Edwin had already been lying awake for a while. He hurt inside and yet felt freer than before. The prior evening had led to deeper self-exploration and it hadn't been easy. Even though he didn't like the process he decided he would trust Percival, and set aside his personal inclinations to get onto the 'good stuff' as he described it. Then he realized the only way to make it more enjoyable and less frustrating was to see this process as part of getting to the good stuff. In fact it is part of the good stuff. He hadn't realized it before."

Sometimes a useful role for a mentor can be to help us solve a business or similar type of life problem. Edwin brought Percival along to help in his pursuit to clear his servant Jaffa from a serious charge:

"Hmmm,' the Sheriff said as he pondered this new development. 'I must say you are right in saying they are much the same. What are your thoughts on the matter, Percival?'

'Yes, I would say the alphabet characters Edwin has pointed out are very similar. Indeed to the point where it could be said they are written by the same person. Also notice how the writing is imprinted fairly deep in the parchment. Deeper than I would say most people write. The bill of sale reflects the same imprinting."

Sometimes a mentor can save us from doing something really damaging as noted in the following excerpt from Evansing:

"He felt this ache for Greer, 'Oh to be back home.' After a while Edwin noticed there didn't seem to be any servants around. 'Strange, where'd they go?' He passed it off and carried on in their conversation. After a while she sat next to him. She rubbed his arm and looked increasingly appealing, in fact she looked gorgeous. He patted her hand she had on his arm. It felt very fine. Now he held her hand on his arm. He looked at her in the way he had only looked at Greer before. The brakes seemed to be coming off. The train seemed to be picking up speed as they both started to get that look. Then they were kissing.

Then they were touching and grabbing, and then…'STOP!' went off in Edwin's head. He stopped, startled. 'What was that?' he thought to himself or so he thought, but he actually said it with his outside voice.

His playmate asked him, 'What's what?' irritated their progress had stopped.

'A voice went off in me that said 'STOP!' 'And I am going to stop. I should never have let this happen in the first place. You are a wonderful young lady and may you find a new husband, but it's not me.' He got on his jacket and left without further ado.

When he arrived back at the home that were his quarters in Randar he was greeted by Percival waiting for him.

'Percival, it is so good to see you. What brings you here?'

'You do.'

'Oh and in what specific way?'

'An officer friend of yours and I do emphasize friend, let me know you were seeing a certain lady tonight, who he had noted seemed to be unduly interested in you.'

If the light had been brighter, then Percival may have noticed Edwin blushed at the revelation of this episode with Faro.

'Ohh really, Percival,' replied Edwin. He dismissed the thought of trying to discredit this as idle thoughts by the officer in question. He knew Percival would not be thrown off by deception.

'Yes, really, Edwin. You could have done serious damage to your relationship with

Greer. If I hadn't yelled 'STOP', who knows where your little visit would have ended up?"

In summary working with a mentor can be very rewarding and even essential to achieve your life goals. Having a wise person who has a heart to give us their best because they want to see us succeed is an invaluable resource. An important part of this is to treat a mentor with honor and respect so as ensure the relationship will flourish and last a long time. Thoughtful gifts and considerations should certainly be a part of this.

# Purpose – Part 1
## Chapter Seven

King Erith, the King of Evansing, had a vision to unite all the Irish kingdoms into one kingdom. This was his life purpose. He knew it would create discomfort and involved a high measure of risk to himself and his kingdom. Nevertheless he decided the purpose was worthy of the sacrifice. The purpose fulfilled would establish a prosperous and peaceful Ireland. He required his subjects and his allies to get on board with his goal. He especially required his officers and leaders in his kingdom to be aligned with this objective. They too must at a heart level embrace the call to unite Ireland in spite of all the challenges to achieving it. They knew it meant being away from home, fighting battles, some of them would die and great resources would be expended to achieve it. Yet they considered it worthwhile to pursue something greater than themselves. They resolved it was a worthy pursuit and Ireland and its people would be better for it.

As it was for the Kingdom of Evansing and its allies, so it is for every person to decide whether they want to live life focused on comfort and safety or on fulfilling their life purpose. Everyone has an inner yearning to fulfill something beyond their everyday life. Many aren't aware that this is what the gnawing is deep inside. Instead it is misdiagnosed as a need missing in their life such as a new relationship or more stuff or whatever else it takes to distract themselves from it. Everyone has been designed to fulfill their own particular purpose. It requires pursuit.

Purpose is defined as the reason for which something is done or created or for which something exists. Closely aligned with our purpose is our genius. The two are inseparable because without our ability to achieve our purpose there is frustration. Therefore an important clue to our purpose are those abilities we are both skillful at and for us feel very natural and easy.

It could be argued that Winston Churchill's ultimate life purpose was to lead Britain during WWII. All his life's challenges led and prepared him for this defining role for which he is most remembered and beloved. It could be argued his life to that point had all been preparation for that critical juncture in history. Churchill himself had a strong sense of destiny. He demonstrated great bravery on the various battlefields while a young soldier. He did not believe he would die before his destiny had been fulfilled.

Our life purpose and genius combined will also work to bring us to the attention of influential people who can further us along that path of purpose to its fulfillment. As Edwin discovered his warrior abilities were important to Erith and Percival but they weren't the only requirements for his being called to be part of the Quest to unite Ireland. See the following:

"Notice of you came to us that you were a great warrior and by you coming to our kingdom we would be able to enhance our warrior capacity. You are a most unusual young man to the degree you have demonstrated personal courage and resolve. Now that you have experienced a personal shift in your desire to grow and be a person of nobility, we have need of your influence. You can create a class of noble warriors in my kingdom."

Fulfilling ones purpose will also require one to handle hard things. King Erith encountered this on a personal level and Evansing faced this on a kingdom level. In order for the mission of unifying Ireland to succeed there needed to be absolute unity amongst his leaders. The following occurred with one of his closest government ministers:

"One of the government ministers ventured to speak up saying, Sire, I must admit I have struggled with the rightness and the difficulty of the task before us. For us to impose our will on the rest of Ireland for their benefit is indeed going to be an arduous task. Is it right for us to be committed to forcing our will on peoples that want nothing to do with us? I am troubled thinking many of those people don't know us nor are even interested in getting to know us. For us and the different peoples across this Isle, the only things we have in common are a Celtic heritage expressed in a myriad of ways and we share the same island.'

The King looked intently and then replied, 'Fenwick, do you have any suggestions as to how we could proceed which would engage your heart in this pursuit of Irish unity?'

'No, Sire, because I am not convinced about the fundamental rightness of the cause.'

'Okay then do I have your word you will not try to in any way interfere with this goal?'

'Yes, Sire, you have my word on it. My loyalty is not at stake here. I will support you in whatever way I can. I would never oppose you or work to undermine you.'

'Okay then I believe you, Fenwick, and you are dismissed for now. I will reassign you to a less strategic role in the government.'

Fenwick arose and left without further comment.

The King then asked again if anyone else was having wavering thoughts about Irish unity and the rightness of their cause to pursue it.

Again, silence.

The meeting continued on into the late afternoon until the King was satisfied with the initial work accomplished.

Greer came to the doorway of the room saying, 'Father, something dreadful has happened. Fenwick was found hanging from his window over the northwest wall, an apparent suicide.'

The King's face became dark with grief and horror. Fenwick had been a long-time faithful and competent government minister. The King even considered him a friend to the extent a king can consider a non-royal a friend.

This sudden turn of events was unfortunate. It could be considered by some as a possible murder by the King's men. There were men who thought the King should not brook those who could not give wholehearted support. This was a ticklish matter for the King as he did not want to be a tyrant over his people. The idea of imposing his kingdom and its allies' will on non-cooperative parts of Ireland challenged his sense of what was right. After much wrestling he had come to the conclusion the overall good to be gained was sufficient to justify the inevitable loss of life and property. As well it justified the imposition of the will of a united Ireland where necessary. He had settled it and he would not re-visit it."

# Purpose – Part 2
## *Chapter Eight*

Passion is an integral part of purpose. Without it the obstacles will prove to be too great and progress will slow or stop. To keep our passion fueled we must seek to stoke our joy. Our joy levels are an important indicator of our passion and our passion levels are an indicator of our joy. Passion combined with genius and purpose will create intense focus. Life has many diversions and if our focus is diffused it will impair our ability to accomplish our purpose. The development of a laser focus is imperative. Along with this is the need for wisdom to know when to shift to take care of other important areas of our life. Take note of the following interchange between Edwin and Greer as they are making wedding preparations:

"Edwin, I have now finished designing my wedding dress and my seamstress has already started. I shouldn't have left it so late, but she assures me she will get it done. Of course you won't be able to see it until our wedding day. Have you selected your outfit yet?'

'Uhh no, as a matter of fact I haven't.'

'Edwin! You are going to have to focus more time on the wedding preparations. I have done most of it already, but there are some things you and I need to discuss. Besides I want it to be us deciding not just me. We can decide together on your outfit. What are you doing this afternoon?'

'Well I had this afternoon free, but Percival and I have just received some news about the Druid we've been looking for. We need to meet with your father and discuss a plan of action.'

'Hmm, it figures. You know sometimes you have to put us first.'

'Greer, this is a matter of top state security. What would your father think if I were to miss this meeting to go check out a wedding outfit?'

'I don't care what he would think. There will always be something which has to be attended to. This wedding has to hit the top of your priority list or else there won't be a wedding."

Fortunately for them both Edwin did make changes in his schedule.

Fulfilling our purpose will require absolute commitment and some things will need to be sacrificed. However as long as you have created the right priorities you will be able to maintain a consistent flow of progress in its achievement. Self-management or as it is frequently called, time management is a required skill consistently exercised. An important component of this is the planning of our lives. One specific technique is to schedule our productive activities in blocks of at least one to two hours. Smaller tasks could be grouped into 30 minute blocks. This way we devote sufficient time to be wholly engaged and get something of consequence accomplished. When we keep bouncing back and forth between emails, phone calls or glancing at this and that it breaks our rhythm and robs us of our productivity. It can take as much as 10 or 15 minutes to get back to the same level of focus and con-centration when we get distracted. Not only productivity but quality can suffer. To avoid being distracted it is important to have a high level buy-in as to what you are pursuing. There must be a great passion that refuses to be denied. Visualization of the goals achieved and the benefits received not only for self but for others can help keep us on track. Daily thanking out loud of goals and their benefits being achieved can stim-ulate us to internalize our purpose as al-ready attained. This builds confidence to keep going when it is hard.

How do we stoke our joy? One major way is to be grateful for virtually every step of progress and every seeming setback. I say "seeming" because setbacks prepare us for the success we are progressing towards. In his pursuit of the light bulb, Edison did not consider his 10,000 experiments as failures but rather as discoveries of ways that did not work. We must look at what appears at first to be a failure as actually a necessary step for progress and preparation for our eventual success. Then we will maintain a joyful outlook which in turn will fuel our necessary passion.

Edison did not consider himself as working but rather considered himself as having fun. This is another integral part of what is necessary to fulfill purpose. If pursuing our purpose is a drudge then either we are mistaken as to our purpose or we have simply let the contrary things rob us of the fun factor. We must look for opportunities to create fun in our daily lives for it refreshes our spirits and enlivens our thinking. When we are having fun we also attract positive relations with others who are necessary for the accomplishment of our purpose.

# Courage – Part 1

## *Chapter Nine*

Courage and strength are essential to living a successful life. Without these qualities the problems of life will wear us down and cause us to abandon or avoid what is necessary for fruitful and meaningful lives. In the following excerpt from Evansing we note Carson's willingness to take on something difficult:

"News of this young boy missing especially touched Carson. He'd had a close call with his eight year old brother the year before. He remembered the torment his family went through when his brother had wandered into the forest. The searchers found him three days later in a very dehydrated condition. His little brother would not have lasted another day.

So with great resolve to make a difference, Carson first went to the parents to ask for some information regarding their son. They were ambivalent about talking to someone from Evansing, but their love for their son overcame their prejudices. Carson gleaned that their son liked to go into the nearby streams. Together they studied drawings of where the streams were located and a description of the terrain. They weren't deep or fast streams, but if Josh had gone into one he could lose the hunting dogs engaged in the search. It seemed as though Carson had a sixth sense about where Josh had gone, for he headed in a direction where nobody considered looking. It was a particularly forlorn area and difficult to enter. The entry though was a stream that wound its way through the middle of that area."

As we note it was with "great resolve to make a difference" that Carson undertook a difficult and as we later discover, a dangerous mission to rescue the missing boy. Courage and strength will always be necessary to engage the tasks or processes necessary to refine us to be who we need to be in order to create a large life. In the course of doing the difficult the hidden treasures that lie within us come to the surface. New genius is discovered which leads to the joy that comes from the satisfaction realized.

Cultivating joy is an important component of being strong. The ancient Hebrews had a saying "the joy of the Lord is my strength." We all feel able to do most anything when we are in a positive frame of mind and emotions. Joy is an integral part of this. Getting focused on something good or perhaps dancing in our cubicle, whatever it takes, are useful for restoring joy.

Facing our fears is a way to build our courage to do the tasks or pursue the projects that may at first even appear to be impossible. This doesn't mean that you take on the giants in the land right off the bat. It may simply mean you join a Toastmasters group and begin speaking on a regular basis in front of a group of people. This will build your courage and strength levels as it is commonly stated that public speaking is one of the most common fears. Another way is take on a leadership position in an organization. This extra pressure will strengthen your inner being resulting in a new ability to take on even greater challenges. A key here is to get relatively comfortable with discomfort. In other words embrace the discomfort. You choose to value the benefits of the desired outcome as more important than the discomfort experienced to achieve it.

Here we have a major stumbling block to great achievement. Often people want to achieve greatness without the pain and discomfort of the journey to get there. That is living in a fantasy.

What would we think of an explorer in the 1700s in North America who didn't like the idea of being uncomfortable? Naturally we would think he is being unrealistic and would question whether he should be considering a vocation of an explorer. It's like a missionary being sent to a small village in Africa who doesn't like dirt. The prognosis would not be good for them to stay long.

# Courage – Part 2
## Chapter Ten

Edwin as an effective leader demonstrated courage that inspired his men. Consider the following scene from Evansing:

"Erith's officers briefed him about the casualties and though dismayed at the degree of their losses knew they could have been greater. He had expected them to be at least 25% higher. He had considered the great disadvantage afforded them in having to go uphill. Erith enquired why things turned out as well as they did. Several officers offered the following observation: Troops had been noted as commenting how they had been inspired to dig deeper and fight more fiercely as a result of seeing Edwin charge up the hill. They had seen him battle with such wild abandon and a seeming lack of concern for personal safety. This drove them to another level of courage and boldness."

Followers want leaders they can respect and who will inspire them to be all they can be. Effective leadership requires the courage and strength of character necessary to make tough decisions in spite of the risks.

An interesting aspect of focusing on growing our strength and courage is that it tends to minimize our susceptibility to being discouraged or otherwise negatively affected by discomfort. As these qualities grow there is a greater reserve to roll over those experiences that previously would have slowed us down or perhaps stopped us completely.

Qualities of strength and courage will result in you attracting like people as Edwin did in the following excerpt from Evansing:

"The evening ended well with Edwin making some new acquaintances and perhaps at least one new friend. The new friend was the third ranking military man in Nerland. He was not much older than Edwin being only in his mid-twenties. Like Edwin he had demonstrated amazing leadership and courage. They both seemed to click with one another as soon as they had met."

Creating alliances and partnerships with such people will increase your likelihood of creating the critical mass of genius necessary to accomplish prodigious success.

Erith the King of Evansing had a close friendship with a very wise and loyal friend, Percival. Many times Erith would draw upon the wisdom and emotional support of Percival. He knew the call he had been given was a difficult one. In order to maintain the courage to face the obstacles he needed someone he could trust and who had only his best interest at heart. Also he needed someone willing to confront him when necessary. Percival was such a man. Of course it meant that both men shared the same view of the quest to unite Ireland. They both believed it to be worth the sacrifice required. Together they could fuel each other with the encouragement necessary to maintain the courage. A friend who really believes in you and what you are pursuing, especially when few do, is an invaluable resource in any large undertaking. If you have such a friend already then treat them like gold. By that I mean regularly demonstrate your appreciation and how you value their friendship. Ensure they are gaining value from their friendship with you. If you don't yet have such a friend then start to look out for possible candidates to fulfill such a role. They may already be a part of your circle of influence or they may yet to be met. To ascertain if part of the former, it would be good to review your circle of influence and see who possibly could fulfill that role. This sort of search requires finesse as it balances friendship with looking for someone to take it to the next level of support in your life. Of course the most direct and perhaps simplest approach is to hire a business/executive/life coach to work with you. A good coach will ask the hard questions and make you accountable in ways that most friends never will.

In closing, an important discipline is to ask yourself whenever you are faced with a decision, are you making a choice based on fear or comfort or convenience? Or are you making a decision based on courage?

# Obstacles Can Be Removed
*Chapter Eleven*

I noted the above in the way I did because it certainly needs emphasis. Often we cringe when obstacles are noted on the road ahead. Even the relentless achieveaholics who seem to overcome every challenge before them have their moments of self-doubt and questioning whether they can do it. The key is they do it. They don't get bogged down in giving in to those negative thoughts and feelings. They more often than not anticipate the obstacles and have already created an internal reference point for dealing with them. As well they are more moved by the rewards of objectives attained rather than to the stress of dealing with obstacles.

Edwin showed a remarkable confidence in dealing with obstacles, even when quite unknown. Notice his initial "plan" to enter Grange and kill the wicked Druid:

"Great! Thanks, Percival. Now for my plan, mind you I haven't really thought about it in any great detail. I haven't thought about it in any detail other than this: You turn into a big bird, I jump on your back, we fly to Grange and we take out the bad guy."

Of course, Percival reins in his youthful boisterousness with the following:

"That's about how detailed I thought your plan would be. Hmm, I think we need to consider some additional thoughts on the matter. One matter is how we approach Grange without being detected. Brydon is sure to have ways of picking up any movements towards him."

In this interchange Percival displays the value of having someone with a different perspective. He is not dismissing Edwin's plan. Rather he is adding to it. In the ensuing conversation they both ask the necessary questions so as to cover additional areas of concern needing to be addressed. Edwin's original "plan" could have been character-ized a bit reckless, but through the helpful guidance of an older mature friend it be-came much more balanced and prudent.

An important determinant as to how we face obstacles is confidence. A definition of confidence is as follows: the feeling or belief that one can rely on someone or something; firm trust. People who face obstacles with confidence know they can rely on another person or persons and/or their own abilities to overcome. To rely on other people would require the building up of trust through relationship and experiences which con-firmed their trustworthiness. As well when trusting in one's own abilities most likely there has been a history of success that assures them they can do it. In some cases people have a strong sense of confidence through the right encouraging words from a significant person or persons in their life. This is normally when a person is a child. This gives definite support to being careful what you say to your children and grandchildren. Your words can propel them to success or failure depending on their content. It may give them confidence to do just about anything, even if they have never done it before. We can do the same to ourselves by nurturing our spirit through positive confirmations spoken over ourselves in a manner that expands our view of what we are capable of doing. Expressing words of gratitude as though the objective is already achieved are especially useful for building confidence. The power of gratitude is dealt with in greater detail in Chapter 12, but I would like to emphasize how significant gratitude is for overcoming obstacles. Being grateful and expressing it wholeheartedly increases our sense of well-being. This in turn increases our sense of what is possible. Likewise we can impart this to other people, sometimes seemingly by accident. For example, J.J. Watt, now a star player in the NFL was asked by a young boy "what are you doing delivering pizza?" At the time Watt had given up on pursuing his dream of playing college football after being rejected as too small. Watt responded to this challenge by working out with ferocity to add the additional pounds, strength and speed to get into the college where he wanted to play football. When we see someone struggling below their potential we can speak the right words to ignite them to change for the better.

One typical feature of an obstacle is that it almost always appears bigger and more impossible than the reality. I am now re-peating some information from a previous chapter. When David faced Goliath it was only after the Israelite army was too afraid to battle the giant. David looked at Goliath as an opportunity to win tax free status for his family and the hand of King Saul's daughter. To him Goliath looked like a very inviting target for his slingshot. He even ran toward the giant without a sword and said he was going to cut his head off. He did cut his head off and with Goliath's own sword. Two different perspectives were at play in this situation. The army of Israel was convinced Goliath was unbeatable and even though a very generous reward was at stake, the fear of death was a greater disincentive than the incentive to fight. David had a different perspective. As already noted, he saw Goliath as a ticket to a new life. By slaying the giant he became a national hero. He had great confidence in his skills and he had the courage to try something no one else would. Notice too how he also spoke in a way that would further enhance his courage as he ran toward the giant. Surely the onlookers must have thought David had lost it. But no, with bold audacity and skill he won himself the King's rewards and a place in history.

We may not encounter those kinds of opportunities. But one thing is certain to leap forward in life we will have to overcome obstacles. Our perspective could make all the difference in our winning in grand style or forfeiting an opportunity to dramatically change our lives for the better. Fulfillment of our destinies will require our willingness to risk and do what no one else is willing or able to do.

As noted with David he was prepared. He had practiced his skill with his slingshot. He had slain both a lion and a bear trying to take his sheep. The former trained his practical skills and the latter developed his confidence and courage to face difficult challenges and win. Both were vital in the development of his ability to bravely take on a battle no one else was willing to fight. So it is for each one of us. We must ensure we have done our best to hone our skills and have made efforts to develop our capacity to remain calm and confident under difficult circumstances. In both cases working with a knowledgeable coach could be essential to developing what we need to overcome the obstacles. A competent coach can provide an objective influence to encourage us to develop the needed skills. Also they are able to help with the internal work for greater confidence and courage so we can accelerate our capacity to successfully face that next big opportunity disguised as an obstacle.

# Wisdom – Part 1
*Chapter Twelve*

Wisdom is a prerequisite to a successful life. In order to develop and grow wisdom a person must actively pursue it. One powerful way to pursue is to observe and study people who are renowned for wisdom in your field of endeavor; reading writings about them, if possible hearing them speak or by whatever other means to observe and study their ways of doing things. These could go a long way to establishing a level of wisdom that would otherwise take many years to establish. For example the renowned Napoleon Hill went around interviewing numerous successful businessmen and in a relatively short time was able to distill their wisdom to use in his own life and profitably share with the world in his own book, "Think and Grow Rich."

In Evansing we see the ongoing wisdom Edwin gained from his sessions with Percival:

"The next morning, Percival and Edwin met to see about strengthening some of his internal moral structures.

Percival began, 'Moral frameworks are strengthened by consistently making the right choices. As a consequence, no matter what the circumstances are, we continue to make the right choices. This means we must make right decisions, even in seeming little things. For if we haven't established a mind-set of how to deal with what appears to be the minor areas of life, we will have no moral reserve to draw upon when major temptations come upon us.'

'This talk of strengthening is a bit premature in your case, Edwin. Due to the deplorable lack of proper parental guidance, the moral structures weren't put there in the first place. You can't strengthen what isn't there. So therefore, we need to develop in you what should have been deposited in you as a child. Not a small thing. You have had no problem with being faithful to Greer, because you have been so smitten by her. And because she has always been nearby except for short absences. Then the circumstances changed, so you weren't naturally protected. Now you were on your own. Without an internal compass as to how to respond to an interested attractive woman, you were pretty much at the mercy of what your hormones and emotions wanted to do. We must establish in you such a rock solid, non-negotiable sense of loyalty to Greer. This is so no matter how justified you are feeling, or how rough your circumstances, or how appealing the woman, you will stay the course of marital fidelity.'

'Okay, so how do we do this?'

With that the two men spent the rest of the morning delving into Edwin's early years. This resulted in some more snotty-nosed embarrassing weepy episodes but also greater freedom for Edwin. To top it all off, Percival proclaimed some blessings over Edwin. These were designed to create for Edwin new levels of wisdom in his relations with women."

Once again we see the value of a wise and trusted confidante to provide Edwin with much needed wisdom. The process of growing in wisdom can take a variety of paths.

Sometimes wisdom comes from following a path that one finally realizes is not the path they want to be on anymore. In the case of Edwin he had been on a path of being a warrior raider which left him feeling unfulfilled, poor and friendless. As alluded to in Chapter 1 he experienced awareness that there was a different way to live and he acted upon it. This was wisdom. When we experience awareness it is a new form of wisdom that is being birthed provided we act upon it. Wisdom is the wise use of knowledge. In other words a person must apply the knowledge represented by awareness and do it in a way that is the best possible use of that knowledge.

In Evansing there is an encounter between St. Patrick and Edwin that gives additional insights about wisdom:

"As Patrick and Edwin walked back toward the Evansing line, Patrick shared with Edwin greater and greater insights about his future. He told him how he would eventually become a great king over all of Ireland. In order for him to be successful he must have a heart passionate in his pursuit of Wisdom and Understanding.

'How do I grow in wisdom and understanding?' asked Edwin.

'Learn to listen and truly hear what is being said. It is easy to think we hear, but often there are influences which affect the way we hear."

The passionate pursuit and learning how to listen are given as essential aspects in growing wisdom.

First, there is the passionate pursuit of wisdom. In order to become a person of wisdom it will require a dedicated study and pursuit of the subject. This discipline must be combined with the passion necessary to undergo the training demanded in order to grow in wisdom. Without passion the process will be too onerous and the pursuit will stall. Passion provides the juice of flow and acceleration. What would otherwise be drudgery now becomes a joy. How does one create passion for growing in wisdom? One major means is a clear understanding of what wisdom will do for you. By being aware of the benefits you can now focus on how your life will change for the better. Another means is to focus on how you can make a difference in the lives of those special to you. If you still don't feel the passion then it means something deeper is at work. This may require some deep emotional healing and/or the identification of a lie that makes you doubt the benefits of wisdom to you and those close to you.

Secondly, there is learning how to listen. Without careful listening we can miss important pieces of information vital to our achieving a particular objective. This could be closing a sale, making the right decision on a project or appropriately responding to your spouse. A single wrong word can totally change the outcome in an interaction. It is important to listen for clues and cues as to what and who you are dealing with. Practical tips: Put away your smartphone and any other distractions or potential distractions. Suspend the inclination to assume you know what they are talking about and wanting to focus on what you want to say next. Instead stay wholly in the moment with your entire focus on what is being said. This will increase your retention of what was said. As well when you give undivided attention you are demonstrating valuing the other person. This is a way of honoring that person. The information you gleaned by being a careful listener may not be particularly valuable.

However you will gain an increased level of connection with the people important to you. This will translate into increased income, love and health.

# Wisdom – Part 2

*Chapter Thirteen*

Compassion may not seem like an aspect of wisdom, but it most certainly is. When we relate to another human with compassion we have a heightened awareness and sensitiveity to their needs in that moment. This is vital to knowing the appropriate and loving way to respond to them. Again this can make a tremendous difference in a transaction. Not just a commercial trans-action but in all types of transactions between people.

Self-control is a vital component of wisdom. This could be in areas of sexual conduct. It is interesting to note that the book of Proverbs spends a large portion warning against sexual misconduct. We all know of families ripped apart because someone allowed themselves to get entangled in an adulterouss relationship. We need to exercise self-control in matters concerning the opposite sex. Even careers can be ruined by such actions. As well self-control could entail discipline to do what needs to be done in order to achieve the goals necessary to have a successful life. It also could include re-straint in not doing certain things like indulging in excessive eating and drinking or indulging in taking drugs.

Wisdom can come from learning from what doesn't work and from what does. It is unwise to keep acting in the same way hoping the outcome will be different. In business for example, this could be using the same media and ad copy over and over again with no visible results and yet some-how believing it is worthwhile.    To ensure something is truly working there needs to be a way of testing and measuring. When a particular approach can be objectively evalu-ated then it is possible to make an informed decision about whether to continue it or whether to alter it and evaluate again. This could be done a number of times until an approach is identified as being the most profitable. This process would be characterized as wisdom for it is achieving the best possible outcome with information available.

Prudence is not fear or pathological inclination to always look for what is wrong with something but it could be called a healthy skepticism. You want to avoid being a self-confident fool who looks only for information that supports his or her position. It is important to do the due diligence. Try to prove how it can't work. Prudence is a form of wisdom.

There is a trap that many people have fallen into. Being tricked by believing someone is reliable simply because they are a friend of a friend or even a family member. Consequently they don't get outside advice and don't seriously consider whether the opportunity makes sense. Not considering implications of losing money they can't afford to lose, especially if borrowing money. This is unwise.

Wisdom also knows when there is meant to be balance and when there is meant to be extreme. People who are always balanced in their approach no matter what the situation can actually be quite out of synch when matters are requiring a more vigorous response. As well people who are always extreme in how they do things will find themselves creating a lot of life turbulence. This will prove harmful to their relationships and their physical, mental, emotional and financial well-being.

An obvious example of when an extreme response is necessary is if a husband sees someone emotionally or sexually harassing his spouse. I don't mean he needs to be violent unless absolutely necessary but steps must be strong enough to ensure that the spouse knows her husband cares for her and is not afraid to demonstrate it. A mild let's be reasonable approach would not cut it with a wife in that situation.

An example of inappropriate extreme behavior is the person who flies into a rage at every little slight as opposed to maintaining a calm response. Anger makes fools out of even the most intelligent people. Best to learn how to heal the causes of anger so it doesn't ruin you.

How does a person know they are making a decision with wisdom? One way is to consider if the decision you make is likely to hurt or help yourself and/or others. This will require halting the inclination to make a decision based on some force working on you in the moment. It means stopping and considering implications and whether you want to deal with consequences if the decision does not work out well. If you are not confident in your ability to settle this by yourself or the potential implications are quite large then talk to those who will be affected by your decision and others whose input you trust.

Of course you should always discuss significant decisions with your spouse. A good rule to live by is to not go ahead on any course of action your spouse does not agree to.

Certain books of course can be a great source of wisdom. One that I particularly like is "The Richest Person Who Ever Lived" by Steven K. Scott. The sub title is "King Solomon's Secrets to Success, Wealth and Happiness." It's compact and easy to read and filled with nuggets. I remember having it with me in a Starbucks when the fellow next to me noticed I had that book. He commented that of all the books he liked it was the one he kept re-reading every six months or so. I had noted that one of the qualities stressed by Scott was the importance of treating people with honor. A short time later I viewed a video of Scott interviewing two founders of a new health company. He practiced what he preached. I have never seen someone lavish such genuine honor on people.

While we are on the topic of honor it would be well worthwhile to point out that cultivating a lifestyle of honoring people is a very wise way to live. It will go a long way to creating and maintaining strong relationships which will in turn lead to healthier and happier lives. As well it will lead to greater and brighter opportunities.

As noted in an earlier chapter, I remember hearing in a movie preview that "fear rots your brain." Be aware if you are being driven by fear. Decisions based on fear are unlikely to be right and are most likely to be a source of regret. People of wisdom make their best decisions when they are in a state of calm, in spite of circumstances.  Fear is a choice, therefore we have the power to make the right choice. Make choices based on calmly considering the alternatives and possible consequences of each alternative. Consider not only the possible positive outcomes but also the possible negative outcomes of any choices.

# Willingness to Do the Hard Thing – Part 1

*Chapter Fourteen*

A willingness to do the hard thing will set you apart from the average person. As well it will result in you accomplishing things that others tend to avoid. In Evansing, Edwin faced difficult decisions concerning what he felt needed to be shared with King Erith. One of these was when he was convinced Evansing and its allies needed to retreat instead of continuing to do battle.

"Edwin decided he could not wait any longer.

'Sire, may I please talk to you in private for a moment?'

Erith looked quizzically at Edwin and nodded yes. They then both stepped away from the others some distance so as to not be overheard.

'Sire, a strong impression came to me about the time you called for a meeting. This impression indicates there has been a shift in the seasons. As you know we have been very much in a charge and advance mode for some time now to unite Ireland. We have used both military and diplomatic maneuverings to achieve that objective. There has been significant success to date. The impression I got most definitely indicated we are now in a consolidate and hold season. As unpalatable as this may seem to you, Sire, I agree with the proposal made to retreat.'

'Traitor, you are an ungrateful traitor. How could you side with someone who wants to retreat?' replied Erith.

The vehemence of the response took Edwin by surprise. He had expected a strong negative reaction but not this strong. He could feel a wave come over him as Erith spoke to him. Struggling to maintain his composure, Edwin remained silent for a moment.

'So do you have anything to say for yourself, Edwin?' demanded Erith.

'Sire, this is not based on me deciding all of a sudden we should retreat.' Edwin's voice got stronger and indeed firmer as he went. 'This came upon me on its own. It's not an attitude I had been harboring beforehand. One moment I am flat out in charge and advance mode. And the next I am getting this strong impression the times had changed. Percival and I have had discussions about the timing of things. About how there are different seasons in life. To do what may be an excellent thing in the wrong season can be disastrous. If we are no longer in a time for us to continue the active pursuit of the uniting of Ireland, then it is time to stop.

It is as simple as that. I too am much dis-appointed by this turn of events.'

Erith had started to calm down, but he remained quite distressed as to what he heard. This dream to unite Ireland had totally possessed him. To now come to the realization it should be put on hold, even for a while, almost devastated Erith. He con-tinued to glare at Edwin but remained silent. Edwin could tell Erith started to come to some sort of terms with what he had heard. At least Erith's glare had noticeably softened."

As can be seen above, sharing sensitive information with a superior can be difficult if it is known that it will not be well received. However these are the moments, although fraught with risk, which can represent great opportunity to make a meaningful con-tribution to whatever organization you belong to. As well often times the person who initially gets upset at receiving unwelcome news may end up respecting the person who shared it. This is because they recognize it was done from a place of integrity and duty.

Winston Churchill seemed to savor the opportunity of looking for difficult assign-ments. During the Boer War in South Africa he signed on as a journalist to cover the conflict. He ended up being captured after leading the defense of a train being attacked and captured by the Boers. Subsequently he escaped and was wanted dead or alive by the Boers. Then he returned to South Africa to eventually become an officer in a South African cavalry unit and displayed further heroics. Before the Boer War when Churchill had run for political office he had lost. Now as a returning hero he was given the winning election that was previously denied to him. All those hard things he had endured now seemed of no consequence. They launched him to the stratosphere of political office.

A major benefit of doing the hard thing is it builds inner strength. Consequently when we meet difficult challenges in the future we have a new reserve of courage and confidence in handling it. This creates greater ease and higher levels of excellence due to a superior state of mind as we stay calm in the midst of doing what needs to be done. It also develops the discipline for making right choices based on what will produce the best possible outcome, not on simply doing what is easy and expedient. Dennis Waitley in his CD series "Psychology of Winning" quoted the following: "Winners make decisions based on goal achieving rather than tension relieving."

# Willingness to Do the Hard Thing – Part 2

*Chapter Fifteen*

Sometimes the hard thing comes in very mundane situations. For example you are in the midst of trying to get something done that you have kept putting off. Then you get a phone call from a close friend or family member. They are in a bad place and they want to talk. Do you continue to try working while sort of listening but continually wishing they would say good bye? Or do you set aside your work and give them your wholehearted attention? When they hang up and the thought comes to you to consider doing something more; like going to keep them company or bringing something to cheer them up, do you ignore that thought telling yourself you are too busy? Or do you respond to it by doing an act of kindness? These are major hard things or so they seem at the time. However when we miss the opportunity and reflect upon it later we realize how we blew it. We need to grow in awareness when we are passing up a key opportunity to deepen an important relationship. They don't often come at times that are convenient. That is why we need to heighten ourselves to greater sensitivity to those moments so we can rise above our emotions that want us to ignore someone else's problem and focus on our task at hand. This is especially challenging for those personality types like Dominant Directors and Cautious Thinkers who tend to be more task oriented. They need to find ways to curb their natural inclination and step back and recognize the importance of their relationships. If we compared the value of what seemed to be so important to the value of the relationship, we would be appalled at our short sightedness. That relationship investment will pay dividends for years to come. That seemingly important task will be long forgotten.

In Evansing there is an incident already noted in chapter 8 which I am repeating here to spell this out further:

"Edwin! You are going to have to focus more time on the wedding preparations. I have done most of it already, but there are some things you and I need to discuss. Besides I want it to be us deciding not just me. We can decide together on your outfit. What are you doing this afternoon?'

'Well I had this afternoon free, but Percival and I have just received some news about the Druid we've been looking for. We need to meet with your father and discuss a plan of action.'

'Hmm, it figures. You know sometimes you have to put us first.'

'Greer, this is a matter of top state security. What would your father think if I were to miss this meeting to go check out a wedding outfit?'

'I don't care what he would think. There will always be something which has to be attended to. This wedding has to hit the top of your priority list or else there won't be a wedding."

Hard things in marriage are often overlooked. An outsider would consider it as hilarious or tragic sometimes as to what we consider too unimportant to invest an extra few minutes of effort to accomplish. Unfortunately those things we neglect can often create cracks in the relationship so that when something really difficult shows up the relationship can't handle the extra weight. In other words there were no regular deposits in the emotional bank account to offset the withdrawals. This has often resulted in a spouse leaving a marriage when everything appeared to be okay. The spouse being left behind can often be bewildered at what to them has been totally unexpected.

In parenting doing the hard thing could involve incorporating a meaningful discipline even though it makes us unpopular with our children. It is so easy to get caught up with wanting to be popular with our children. It is a temptation that needs to be resisted. After all we are their parent not simply their friend. We have a responsibility to ensure our children become responsible and successful adults with all their physical, mental, emotional and spiritual capacities intact. As ancient wisdom says, "Train a child in the way he (she) should go and when he (she) is old he (she) will not depart from it."

In business there are many opportunities to do the hard thing. If we postpone letting someone go because we don't want to be the "bad guy" then we are foregoing our responsibility. We don't benefit our business or them to allow them to continue in a position that is not suited to their genius. We can still be compassionate and assist them in whatever way is appropriate to get new employment. In Europe there have been instances where governments did not raise the possibility of cutting wages and pension benefits for fear of creating an unpopular backlash. They maintained the status quo and allowed the fiscal morass to get ever larger and more intractable. Now those countries are stretched to their max as to how they are going to finance even the basics of what their citizens expect to be provided. Both the business and the government examples demonstrate the perils of making decisions with only the short-term being considered. Truly wise decisions also consider the long-term. A person's life reflects the quality of their decisions made with the long-term in view. Steven Covey's book "The Seven Habits of the Highly Effective Person" describes this as making a decision with the end in mind.

# Perseverance – Part 1

*Chapter Sixteen*

Perseverance is defined as steadfastness in doing something despite difficulty or delay in achieving success. Certainly King Erith had perseverance in his pursuit of the quest to unite Ireland.

First he had a mindset locked on his goal which refused to accept anything but the ultimate success regardless of what resistance was encountered. As well he put no limit on the time required. He would simply keep at it until it got done. Note the following:

"Both of them had at that time expressed an affinity to the idea of Irish unity. It seemed so out of reach they both dismissed the idea as impossible. Now it was coming up again and this time Erith was determined to make it reality. Keltic could feel Erith's conviction so strongly he started to get very excited at the prospect. Here was an opportunity for them both to pursue something bigger than themselves. Bigger than trying to keep peace in the land and live a good life. It would be difficult, but these were Irish warriors who had iron in their souls. They had stuff of legends. Now here lay an opportunity to create folklore. Only these would be true stories that would leave a multi-generational impact on all of Ireland. No longer would their focus be only on extending a little bit of territory here and there and taking a little bit of booty. They would now start to focus on being benefactors for all of Ireland and all of her citizens. Kings don't typically think like that. But true kings do. True kings know they are given positions of power and influence to benefit people, not simply to enjoy advantageous situations for themselves."

As indicated above, in order to stay the course in a difficult long-term pursuit there needs to be a noble cause which rises far above the ordinary. This attitude only comes from considerable reflection as to what is truly important in life.

In this case we see where Erith had a true ally in King Keltic of Nerland. We all need others to keep us persevering when situations get difficult. Friends, mentors, business associates and family members can all potentially supply us with the encouragement and wisdom to keep us going when we want to quit.

One of the most horrific experiences of perseverance was the expedition to Antarctica led by Ernest Shackleton from 1914 to 1916. For over two years Shackleton and his twenty-eight men endured almost unimaginable hardships. The most remarkable aspect of it was that not a single man was lost. Their ship called "Endurance" got stuck in the ice and sank leaving the entire expedition literally out in the cold. They had no radio contact and the rest of the world had no knowledge of where they were. Shackleton considered the following qualities as important for a polar explorer: "In order of priority, he said first optimism, second patience, third imagination (with which he coupled idealism), and fourth, courage. He thought every man had courage." This is a quotation from an interview with Alexandra Shackleton, the explorer's granddaughter.

Another word for optimism is hope. Without hope it is impossible to keep the fight in such adversity. Shackleton was a giant leader as he had such strong concern for each of his men and demonstrated in practical ways like giving his gloves to a crew member who had lost his. Consequently Shackleton suffered frostbite. He found ways to inspire his crew to believe they could make it. Another quote from the aforementioned interview: "Worsley wrote in his diary, 'however bad things were, he somehow inspired us with the feeling that he could make things better." If you want to be a great leader you need to be able to inspire people. Fan their hope to overcome and accomplish their objective even when faced with great difficulties.

Major fruit of perseverance is maturity of character and joyful and confident hope. These qualities fuel each other. Perseverance produces maturity and hope. In turn maturity and hope produces perseverance. In times when all seems lost and hopeless it may be at least some consolation to know with the right attitude it is producing the special fruit of maturity and hope. This may not just be for you but for the benefit of those whose lives you touch. When you are tempted to give in to discouragement and negativity keep in mind the opportunity you have to model a superior response.

# Perseverance – Part 2
## Chapter Seventeen

In Evansing there is a wedding blessing given as follows:

"Then came Percival's time to bless the new couple. He began, 'In the name of the Father, Son and Holy Spirit I bless you Edwin and Greer with the endurance to stay the course and withstand the pressures life will bring your way. May your thoughts as individuals and as a couple be continually and only filled with what is true, noble, pure, lovely, admirable, excellent and praiseworthy. May your life together consistently manifest the fruit of the Spirit, love, joy, peace, patience, kindness, goodness, faithfulness, gentleness, and self-control."

Notice the qualities that follow endurance: true, noble etc. and love, joy etc. I believe they are important qualities in order for a person to be able to endure. They require an awareness of our thoughts and actions. When we are aware that our thoughts are other than those noted above then we need to act upon that awareness and take steps to ensure we think and act consistently with those qualities.

Of course to talk grandly about perseverance belies the fact that it only comes after a tremendous amount of longsuffering. Most likely years and in many cases years and years of relentlessly putting one foot in front of the other believing breakthrough will come. In the course of staying with it something happens to a person which transforms what was once an easily discouraged and upset individual into one who calmly and confidently faces whatever comes with a deep assurance there is a reason for everything. This assurance adds a noble element to the process of persevering. It gives a person a reward while in the midst of great discomfort and frustration. This awareness empowers a person to keep waiting and keep expecting. I find telling myself regularly I have a deep assurance there is a reason for everything helps me to accept life's reverses with greater equanimity and even a sense that it is ultimately a good thing for it is making me stronger in some important way.

The Celtic Irish warriors of long ago did not have easy lives. Indeed many of them probably had their lives cut short in battle or a violent quarrel. Nevertheless there was a divine quality of perseverance about them as they took what life had to offer without complaint.

Some of the greatest gains are made when a person is facing what seems to be a truly hopeless and impossible situation. The emotions are supporting the sense of hopelessness and it seems like everything will end badly. However this is especially the time when one must doggedly keep oneself in a mode of high expectations. Keeping high expectations will fuel our hope, energy and determination. This all adds up to a sense of well-being which may seem downright crazy given the circumstances. Nevertheless by continuing to do so you are serving notice to the Universe you will not be taken down or out. Your intentions are to succeed and as you continue to step in the direction of your goals you will experience the breakthrough you long for.

In the course of persevering there is also a growth in determination to conquer whatever stands in the way. A human spirit who refuses to quit and envisions success will keep going until the goal is accomplished.

# Right Relationships – Part 1
## *Chapter Eighteen*

Right relationships can make a person's life. Wrong relationships can break a person's life. At the beginning of our story about Edwin we find that he is involved in being a raider of surrounding communities, wreaking havoc and death:

"Edwin's prime means of survival and providing for himself was from booty from the raids. He had little inclination to engage in other activities such as farming or some sort of enterprise which created value for the community. He did hunt however and it became another area where he could excel and provide for himself. By the time Edwin was sixteen he had become in many ways like his uncle. Shortly later his uncle died. Now at age twenty Edwin started to get nightmares of what his future was going to be if he continued on his present path. He would wake up with cold sweats as he experienced the desperation of a life dominated by pain, and the desire to get revenge because of the pain."

It can be surmised from the above that Edwin's relationships had a destructive influence on his way of doing life. Fortunately as we had discussed earlier, he had an awakening which led to new awareness of the possibility of a life different than he had known.

A person needs to be aware of what kind of people are going to help them get where they want to end up. People with no ambition to do better than where they are will not encourage another person to grow and pursue their dreams. They will simply bounce from one experience to another with no sense of direction and purpose to their life. If we spend time with them we too could be aimless and purposeless.

Sometimes what may seem obvious to the observer is not so obvious to the person involved. For example as mentioned in an earlier chapter, Edwin decides it is okay to get friendly with an attractive woman vying for his attention:

"In his mind Edwin is thinking, 'I should get going.' But in his heart he is feeling the attention from this young woman is most delightful.

The other Evansing officers were about to leave and again the same officer came to rescue Edwin. This time Edwin felt a little perturbed at being interrupted. But his sense of duty to be well-rested for tomorrow and of course his loyalty to Greer, prompted him to say good evening and to thank his hostess.

Faro gave Edwin's hand a little squeeze goodbye, which seemed to linger a bit longer than would be considered proper for their relationship."

As we can see Edwin is experiencing some vulnerability but fortunately one of his fellow officers came to the rescue. We need to have good friends who are willing to speak up and set us straight when necessary, even when it isn't what we want to hear. If Edwin was fully aware he would have ensured he didn't see Faro again. However he decides it is in his rights and even part of his duties to see her again:

"During the day he received a message from one of Faro's servants. It contained an invitation to dinner tomorrow. Edwin studied the invitation and considered his options. His first inclination was to say no. But then he considered how Faro rep-resented someone of significant influence. He should act to ensure she and her circle of friends were on good terms with the Evansing government. And Edwin happened to be a significant part of that government. Besides there would be servants there, may-be he should ask Carson to join him. No, maybe not, being Greer's cousin he may not appreciate this was just diplomacy.

During the next day, Edwin found himself looking forward to seeing Faro again. After all she was fun. People would understand that he, a soldier away from home would look forward to spending time in the company of a lovely lady. As he prepared to leave for Faro's house he realized he had missed writing Greer the day before and hadn't written her yet today. He had been writing her every day and now he had missed two days in a row.

'Hmmm, she will understand I've been busy with my responsibilities, maybe I will do it tonight when I get home.'

He stopped himself and chose to be a bit late rather than miss another day. He scrawled a hastily constructed note, his briefest yet to Greer, but at least she will know he still loves and misses her. Then he handed it off to the military courier on his way out.

When Edwin arrived at Faro's home he apologized for being late. But then again with the water clocks being the way they were, who would know for sure how late and even if he was late at all.

Faro had on her best greeting outfit, showing a little more cleavage than Edwin remembered seeing a couple of days earlier. She appeared so glad to see him again and he appreciated her enthusiasm."

As you can probably surmise her enthusiasm and Edwin's appreciation of it led to what could have been a deal breaker in his relationship with Greer. Fortunately for him, Percival was able to intervene and prevent things from going too far. Another example of Edwin having a valuable friend who is willing to be unpopular for his betterment. We all need friends who will protect us from ourselves.

Later we will see where Percival needs to spend time with Edwin to achieve the express objective of freeing him from being so vulnerable to attractive young ladies. When it comes to one's sexuality there needs to be awareness of what damage can happen from wrong relationships. Married people should not flirt with someone other than your spouse or allow yourself to spend so much time with a person of the opposite sex that an unhealthy emotional attachment starts to be formed. Be aware when you are excusing your behavior or even using it as a way to get back at your spouse. For single people don't get physically involved with someone else's spouse. It is simply bad practice and can lead to much pain for both parties.

# Right Relationships – Part 2
*Chapter Nineteen*

Men often do not establish deep significant friendships with other men. They tell themselves that between work and their family there is no time for other involvements. This can be misguided. A man cannot expect his work and family to fulfill all his emotional needs. This may appear to work for perhaps even many years, but there will come a time when the effect of that lack of bonding with at least one other male will become painfully obvious. The kids grow up and move away and perhaps his wife gets much more involved with her friends or maybe even leaves. Now he's alone. He has nobody to talk to other than maybe a paid counselor. Of course the benefits of male friends aren't just when life gets extreme but also to add to the joy of truly connecting to another human male in a deep significant way. This makes one emotionally healthier and able to more effectively husband and father. Reason being he won't be looking to his family to fill his emotional tank. Rather he will be available to fill their emotional tanks. When being in friendship with men look for those who have an openness to delve into deeper issues besides sports or other surface topics. For a friendship to really contribute to a man's well-being it needs depth which will feed his soul. In turn he can feed their soul.

Find friends who have values similar to your own. The last thing you need is a friend who wants to influence you in wrong ways. Ideally you want friends who will inspire you and support you and you will do likewise for them. Hopefully you and your friends will create new opportunities of experience for one another. Of course if you have a family it is important not to neglect them for the sake of your friends. That would defeat at least part of the reason for you to have friends in the first place.

Being skillful in relationships does not come naturally for most people. Even the Interactive Socializer (IS) types can learn how to be more effective in relationships. For example an IS personality will have a natural tendency to talk a lot and a lack of ability or willingness to genuinely listen. This may work for a while and they may well be the life of the party, but they won't form deep relationships. This is due to the fact that the best way to demonstrate our valuing a person is by giving our undivided attention when they are talking to us. The other personality types have their own particular set of challenges when it comes to most effectively and appropriately relating to people. Dominant Directors (DD) tend to value getting the task done above how they are treating their people working on the task. This can create resentments among the employees and thus decrease morale and productivity. Therefore the very end of objective desired by the DD leader, fulfillment of the task, will actually be thwarted by his insensitivity to his staff. Social Relater (SR) personalities are highly loyal and seek to maintain harmony in relationships. Carried to extreme this can result in an SR leader unwilling to make the tough decision to let someone go even when it would be in everyone's best interest for them to do so. For the Cautious Thinker the tendency is to focus on a task being done perfectly. This could lead to expecting people to be perfect and lead to unrealistic standards being imposed upon their relationships.

Maintain an attitude of gratitude for those important people in your life. A useful exercise would be to review all the blessings associated with each of those relationships and consider the life time value they represent. By doing so it will create a greater awareness of their value to you. This should result in you being more thoughtful and more excellent in how you treat them. This means not viewing them as an irritation or interruption or getting impatient with them because they aren't perfect in how they treat you. There is always room for improvement in our relationships. Take the initiative to do so.

# Joy – Part 1
## *Chapter Twenty*

Joy is an emotion that we all desire to have as a dominant state but it often eludes us because of life's circumstances that inter-fere. It doesn't have to be that way. We can take control over our joy. We don't have to wait until it just comes on us.

First, we need to know why it is important to us and therefore why it is essential for us to make an effort to maintain joy as our normal state or as I heard one speaker say, "Joy is meant to be our default setting." Joy has a great therapeutic effect on our bodies, minds and of course on our emotions. We are physically, mentally and emotionally healthier when we are in a state of joy. I don't mean it has to be some ecstatic state, it can be subtle yet it is there, a strong sense of well-being which can be characterised as joy. Joy enhances the function of our physical bodies and our minds function at a sharper level. When we are joyful we are easier to be around and our relationships flourish. When we are joyful we perform our work at a higher level with greater creativity and greater attention to detail.

What is a key to joy? Passion about life is a key to joy. Read the interchange between Greer, Princess of Evansing and Kerris, Crown Prince of Alder:

"So tell me what makes you think you would be good for Athandra? I need to tell you right now she has a zest for life, which could shake your world. She is a rather unusual girl in the degree and wide range of things she feels passionate about. So if you want to connect with her you will need to grow in your capacity to be passionate, first and foremost about her and also about life. She loves life. Even though life can be difficult, there needs to be a mindset of embracing difficulties as times of growth. They force out or at least if we allow them to do so, force out to the surface the true self existing deep within us. Passion requires our true self to be visible and engaged with the world.'

Kerris looked amazed at this young woman not much more than a girl who shared this truth he knew to be great wisdom. 'Wow if I can tap into being consistently passionate there is nothing I can't do and I know that my life will shift from being a bore to being a joy. So how do I get there? How do I become this focused lover of life?"

Subsequently Kerris is introduced to Percival who helps him identify a major reason for his lack of passion:

"That evening in Kerris' quarters the two men talked about various things Kerris re-membered from his childhood. They seemed to have an adverse effect on his capacity to enjoy relationships and life in general.  One of the things which seemed to come up as a big issue concerned the matter of performance. All his life Kerris had been rated on the basis of how he did things. Seldom did he feel like anyone celebrated him for being Kerris, beautiful just for being here and alive. He felt like being the perfect Crown Prince was all that mattered to people."

Getting off of the performance treadmill is not easy if that is where you have been for a long time, but it is essential for a true sense of well-being. We all need to know we have value apart from what we do. If we don't, everything in life is just another part of the pressure to perform. It will exhaust and drain our souls of any capacity to be passionate about life. There needs to be a simple joy in just being who we are.

One insight that recently came to me was how every aspect of our current lives are an integral part of our lives and are meant to be embraced as meaningful and related to as having redeeming properties which make them valuable. When we do this it shifts our perspective from considering certain actives-ties as a waste of time or simply as an irritation to be endured, to one where we appreciate each role in our lives as an essential element and therefore to be em-braced and enjoyed. As a result we will have a greater level of focus on the task at hand. This then leads to at least some element of passion which increases our performance level and ability to enjoy even the most mundane of activities.

Another motivation to be joyful comes from recognizing we are not an island. We impact people whether it is at Starbucks while purchasing a coffee from an employee or whether we are in our most intimate mo-ments with those we love. We can make a difference for better or for worse simply by the level of joy or lack of it in our lives. Joy can make a measurable difference to the people we encounter. We can leave a deposit of positive energy that encourages and fuels someone else's day and perhaps even their life. We don't recognize how powerful we are for good or for evil in the lives of others. We need to grow in awareness of toxic thoughts. Toxic thoughts could be simply defined as those that do not encourage joy. Focusing on that which is true, noble, right, pure, lovely, admirable, excellent and praiseworthy will go a long way toward fostering our joy. Another way to view the power of joy is to envision how you want people to remember you. Joy is a powerful building block for a positive legacy. The joy people experienced when they were around you will stay in their memories for a life time. I know for me I had two grandmothers who both died when I was six years old. I also had a step grandfather who died when I was eighteen. I fondly remember him and one of the grandmothers because there was a joy in the relating with them. They demonstrated genuine joy in being with me. They left a positive legacy in me. It enhanced my self-esteem knowing such vital people really cared for me and showed it. They probably didn't always feel good and perhaps they didn't always relate to me in a positive way, but I don't remember any actions by them not positive toward me. I choose to believe they made an effort to be joyful in their demeanour when they were with me. Consequently they left an indelible imprint of good in my life.

# Joy – Part 2

## Chapter Twenty One

Stirring up our hope is a vital way to increase our passion and consequently our joy. A very effective way to stir up hope is to be grateful. As we express gratitude for what we have it turns on a light inside us which leads to joy. When we do our lives from the perspective of gratitude and anticipating good things it adds lightness to our day. It is like we are expecting a happy surprise.

Another key aspect of creating and maintaining joy is having a long term perspective on our lives. Certainly it can be difficult to live in a state of joy if we are unduly impacted by the ups and downs of everyday life. One moment it seems great and only getting better. Next moment something unexpectedly bad happens or perhaps in some ways even worse, life keeps droning on in a mundane way without the exciting breakthrough we are hoping for. Whatever it is, we need to know these momentary experiences can change by a single phone call or new idea. The important thing is not to let our current situation block our ability to keep our eyes on our anticipation of long term good in our lives. Often adverse circumstances, if we allow them to, can become important building blocks in our character creating the long-term success we are longing for. While we have breath there are undreamt possibilities still available to us. Maintaining a joyful anticipation is a necessary key to accessing those possibilities.

When we are in a difficult place being joyful may even seem ludicrous. It is in times like those that joy is especially important to keep our morale up and maintain our capacity to perform at high levels.

I remember reading a passage where though a writer painted a very dismal set of circumstances he is yet "turning cartwheels of joy." I find this fascinating as it is an example of supreme determination to do whatever it takes to regain joy. I can't physically do cartwheels but I can do my version of cartwheels which stirs up a connection with joy. I will twirl my finger as though I am doing cartwheels. For me it ignites my joy because it connects me to this passage. Often a physical action can be used to stir something up in us. In this case it's joy. Each one of us needs to find what we can do to activate our joy. Looking at heartwarming pictures of grandchildren or getting on our bicycle and going for a vigorous ride are other examples of physical actions we could do to regain our joy. Whatever we do it is important to do something and not just resign ourselves to a state of not being in joy. When we feel tired and depressed nothing seems to work. But when we are energized and joyful, things flow and tend to work out.

# Gratitude

*Chapter Twenty Two*

As noted in Chapter 1 practicing gratitude increases awareness. This in turn makes conceivable our limitless thinking. There is an important reason why this is so. By cultivating gratitude as our normal state we expand our internal sense of what is possible, regardless of seeming obstacles. Everything worth pursuing has obstacles. Therefore it is important to cultivate an attitude in our pursuit of a worthwhile objective which increases our assurance of overcoming all obstacles. There is actually a physiological basis to this as well. Expressing heartfelt gratitude for all manner of things increases our joy levels and sense of well-being. This translates into shifts in our body that increases our energy levels. Increased energy gives us greater capacity to take on difficult tasks and not be easily distressed or discouraged. It also empowers us to see good where before we only saw loss or disappointment. Gratitude increases the ability to enjoy life regardless of circumstances.

Focusing on gratitude increases awareness and magnetizes our capacity to attract new people into our life. New opportunities most frequently arise in our lives through relationships. There is a natural aspect as well as a mystical aspect to this attraction. By having a dominant demeanor of gratitude it makes us more pleasant to be around. Successful people are attracted to positive vibes and there are few things that create more positive frequencies than gratitude which is expressed. Direct expression of appreciation and gratitude to the favors extended to you by others is of course always greatly appreciated and encourages more of the same. Look for ways to lavish the appreciation in a sincere manner. This is so as to fully impart to the other party that truly you have been impacted and want them to know the full measure of your pleasure. People crave to be appreciated. One of the most productive ways of engaging other people is looking for opportuneities to express heartfelt gratitude. We should all want to grow in awareness of every blessing bestowed on us by others and then look for ways to acknowledge it. Not always just with verbal expression, but sometimes a card and even a suitable gift could make an impact not soon forgotten.

In Evansing, Edwin especially demonstrates gratitude for his new situation in life. He doesn't take it for granted. He knows he is fortunate and his actions towards people display kindness and care. His gratitude increases awareness of his good fortune. This in turn creates a greater naturalness to treat others in a manner that is akin to one wanting to give other people a reason to be grateful. In other words your benefiting them in some way is designed to create in them an attitude of gratitude for your blessing them.

A major benefit from regularly practicing gratitude is that it fends off an attitude of ingratitude. Ungrateful people tend to be complainers, easily irritated, low performers and generally hard to deal with. They are always looking for what is in it for them. Their normal state is to be stingy and un-willing to assist others without expecting some sort of direct pay back. If being grateful had no other benefits aside from counteracting the qualities of ingratitude then that would be reward enough.

If being grateful and thankful is a challenge for you then I would recommend the cultivation of it becoming one of your greatest pressing priorities. You could start off with expressing thanksgiving for basic blessings like air to breathe, food to eat and a place to lay your head. If even that is a challenge then simply say over and over "thank you." Don't let negative emotions and lies bombarding you tell you that you have nothing to be grateful for. I guarantee your demeanor and your life will change with consistent and persistent expressions of "thank you" in one form or another.

Another way to stimulate an attitude of gratitude as your normal view of life is regularly tell yourself how fortunate you are. Here again you may be bombarded with "You are crazy to say that or even think that." That is perfectly normal. However, those are lies, no matter how seemingly desperate your life has been or is presently. The objective is focus on those areas where you are fortunate and regularly remind yourself of this truth. The fact is many people are way more fortunate than they recognize because they constantly focus on the areas they don't like or wish were different. Consequently they don't acknowledge the areas of their good fortune. As you focus on the areas of good fortune and regularly acknowledge how fortunate you are for those blessings you will see further enhancement in those areas. Then you will start noticing the other areas start shifting for the better as well. Whenever you notice a betterment, no matter how small it may appear to be, ensure you express thanks and celebrate it. By celebrating progress it increases the quality of gratitude. Celebration of something increases the force working to bring it about.

Being thankful has an element of the divine. There is a sacred verse that exhorts the reader to "In all things give thanks." We should regularly recognize all the blessings which we have received without our doing anything to deserve them. As we do so it will awaken our inner selves to a Force in our life far beyond what we see with our physical eyes.

The day that I wrote this passage I was feeling a bit low. Then I realized I needed to review my gratitude journal. By doing so I restored my sense of perspective about my life and I gradually felt mentally and emotionally better. A gratitude journal is simply a place where you record those special blessings to remind yourself that indeed you do have things to rejoice over and be thankful. You will find it a vital way to restore your mental and emotional equilibrium. Of course we all know that as our mental and emotional states go so does our physical state. Regularly expressing gratitude and thanksgiving is like taking vitamins and minerals. It instills in our bodies another level of strength and harmony necessary to function in their designed manner. We all need something to give us a healthy tonic of reality and that is precisely what a gratitude journal will do for you.

Try wording proclamations in a statement of being thankful for it with real heart-felt meaning behind it. I just tried it and noted a profound difference from how I had stated it before. By stating affirmations and goals in a manner of giving thanks for them, it is like it is already done, already received. This adds another dimension of substance to our words which has the effect of increasing the power being released into the atmosphere to support our pursuit of those promises and goals. Not only into the atmosphere but also into our being so deeply it increases our capability to exercise those steps necessary to achieve those objectives.

In conclusion then it would not be over-stating the point to say being grateful and expressing it is one of the most powerful actions we as humans can do. It changes us; it changes people around us and affects our very environment with positive frequencies.

# Hope – Part 1
## Chapter Twenty Three

Hope is one of the essential qualities in life. With it we can leap over tall buildings in a single bound. Without it we have difficulty getting out of bed. Knowing this means it is essential to do those things that will nurture our levels of hope. In Evansing we have the following incident where Edwin encountered hope for the first time:

"As Edwin lay on his bed of straw contemplating these things, a Grey thrush with brown specks on its body came into his hut. The bird seemed not to be afraid at all of Edwin but rather curious and even friendly in his demeanor. Fascinated, Edwin watched the bird and threw it some bread crumbs. The bird pecked away at the bread and chirped in gratitude. Something in Edwin switched on as he experienced warmth in his heart he had not felt for a long, long time. An emotional shift occurred inside him as he realized his act of kindness toward the bird had done something in him as well. He threw the bird some more crumbs and again the bird chirped a happy song of gratitude. The warmth in Edwin's heart became more intense. It startled him for it was so foreign. Then the bird came closer to Edwin. As Edwin slowly extended out his right forefinger to the bird, the bird stopped and watched in silence. Then it hopped several times and landed on the outstretched symbol of friendship. Edwin had made a friend, his first true friend in many years. Edwin noticed hot tears rolling down his cheeks. This was strange, for warriors do not cry and Edwin was in many ways a consummate warrior. The bird remained on his finger with his head bent up looking into Edwin's eyes. He seemed to relax and quite enjoyed being on this unusual perch. Then something unexpected happened. The bird spoke. Or at least it seemed he spoke. Edwin started to get thoughts in his head as though the bird was indeed communicating with his mind. Now in that time of Irish history there were often tales of spirits inhabiting animals and communicating to people. This was different though; this bird was 'talking' to Edwin not to someone else. It didn't seem to be a spirit and certainly not a malevolent spirit.

'How would he know the difference?' Edwin thought to himself.

He didn't except he had this inner knowing.

The bird was telling him his thoughts of going to the monastery were good and he was to ask for a particular monk called Percival. As Edwin pondered what was going on he started to experience something else he had not felt before. He believed it must be what is known as hope.

As he considered this new hope growing in him, the bird seemed to say goodbye and flitted away through the opening in the door. At first Edwin felt a twinge of regret about the abrupt departure. However, he knew what had happened was good, indeed very good."

Here we have an example of where an infusion of hope creates awareness and the courage to act upon that awareness. If a person lacks hope it stifles ability to receive awareness and immobilizes a person from taking action to change their situation. In this case Edwin is now seriously considering a drastic life changing move.

Later on Edwin has been captured by King Taryn of Merethath as a bargaining chip. While he is in a dungeon awaiting his fate he does the following to keep his spirits up:

"Edwin looked away to the wall and started to remember the last time he saw Greer. He would remember her and not let these thugs have the satisfaction of distressing him. In fact he decided he would be happy regardless of where he was. This represented another opportunity for personal growth and greater freedom. He would choose to think and act like a mighty prince.

He started to smile to himself at the prospect of using this time as an opportunity to gain the strength of character Percival intended to do through discussions and reflection. This increased the pressure and forced the process to speed along more rapidly. Good, he was getting a vision for how this could be a good thing. After all, Erith would make a deal for him and he would be out of here probably in a week or two at the most."

Notice how he got a vision of Greer to keep up his spirits. He focused his thoughts on that which brought him happiness. Next he re-characterized his situation as an oppor-tuneity for accelerated growth. Lastly he told himself of how he would likely be freed quickly. These responses all stirred up hope in Edwin for a successful resolution of what was a serious set of circumstances. This hope kept him in a place of internal well-being that his externals couldn't touch. He was literally a prisoner of hope. Therefore he maintained a clear calm mind and could respond in a healthy productive way while in that dungeon.

# Hope – Part 2
## Chapter Twenty Four

Hope is the anticipation of good things. Visualizing a successful outcome is one way of building our hope. Avoid seeing yourself having an unfortunate ending to whatever challenge you are facing. Another way is creating statements affirming a positive result which we can regularly declare over ourselves. Our words have great power for good or evil in our lives. Therefore avoid speaking the things you don't want in your life. Rather speak the things you do want. This can be very demanding on us psychologically for it can seem logical to express distressing thoughts and feelings. It requires an act of the will as we realize it is more important for us to express the outcomes we want even if it seems phony or silly at the time. This is because our inner being is receiving the words as truth even if our mind is struggling with it. Our sub-conscious will progressively respond to the positive words so as to bring about the thoughts and actions required to achieve the desired outcome. The foundation of all this is hope.

Hope gives us the energy to take on new endeavors even when the outcome is uncertain. Ultimately there is an element of hope in every human transaction. We buy something with the expectancy it will fulfill a desired need, we get married believing it will work out and we start a new business with expectancy of success.

Sometimes we can be plagued by a sense of hopelessness due to unresolved hurts as the following from Evansing discloses:

"Edwin this time decided to interject, 'Percival, what can we do to maintain hope and assist others to maintain hope?'

Percival looked a little surprised at the question. 'Why with all you are enjoying and anticipating would you ask me that?'

'I know I have many things to be positive and happy about, but I still have those times when I wonder 'what is the point?' and it makes me feel a sense of hopelessness.'

'That's those deep down hurts still trying to express themselves. When it happens ask yourself why you are feeling that way and what is the root cause. Those emotions are opportunities for freedom. When you can identify the specific causal issue you can take steps to get healed and freed."

The point is to take action when we feel hopeless. We don't want to stay there. It is crucial for us to maintain our hope in life. All good things in life are available when hope is present. Without it the good things in life become elusive. To help us with maintaining hopefulness even when we are encountering negative circumstances, it is imperative we have encouraging hope filled people in our lives. They will fan the flames of our hope. They are another good reason why we want to be circumspect in establishing right relation-ships.

The dictionary definition of hope: "Hope is an optimistic attitude of mind based on an expectation of positive outcomes related to events and circumstances in one's life or the world at large."

Therefore in closing it is important to maintain an expectation of success in whatever we are engaged. That includes situations that are unpleasant and scarily uncertain or even appear impossible. Especially in those kinds of situations we should maintain our hope. This will require us at times to seemingly disengage our minds and simply go with our heart conviction. Ignore those beckoning luring thoughts of fear and worry as you survey your circumstances. Continue to stay in faith expecting all things will turn out well.

# Self-Control

*Chapter Twenty Five*

Self-control is not a glamorous character trait. Yet it is essential to our long-term success. We are all aware of situations where we allowed ourselves to go at least a bit out of control. This frequently happens when it comes to our physical senses. Eating, drinking and sex are all areas where the potential for being out of control can be quite high and where the consequences can be damaging in the short-term and certainly in the long-term. Another major area is finances. Know anybody who spends beyond their means and incurs crushing debt in the process? Unbridled anger can result in broken relationships, injuries and even death.

The above scenarios are rather obvious examples of where being self-controlled in our actions can help us to avoid unfortunate experiences.   The following from Evansing gives a clear example of the benefits of not letting one's temper get the worst of oneself:

"Edwin started on his way with the wind behind him and the sun in his face. It was one of those rare Irish mornings which had more sun than cloud. It seemed to Edwin like even the weather was cheering him on in his decision to change his life. After walking for four miles he came by the house of one of his mother's brothers. Two of his cousins saw him and yelled at him to stay away because he wasn't wanted. Edwin grinned at them and kept walking. A couple of miles later he came by the home of a man who'd had a bitter feud with Edwin's uncle. He swore at Edwin and told him he'd kill him if he had the chance. Uncharacteristically Edwin wished him a top'o the morning and briskly kept walking.

Edwin thought to himself, 'What has happened to me?'

It all seemed so strange. Yesterday he would have been enraged towards his cousins and at the least would have yelled some disparaging words back. And with the man who threatened to kill him, if that had happened yesterday he would have challenged him to sword play with the full intent of killing him."

Edwin neatly sidestepped the temptations presented to him. By doing so he did not divert his focus and energy in an unproductive way. He kept on his path toward the monastery.

Here we have an elevated view of the value of being slow to anger and being able to rule over one's own spirit.

Another area of an important need for self-control is the managing of ourselves. This is frequently called time management. Strictly speaking we can only manage ourselves, not our time. The reason this is so vital is because the years go by quickly and if we get into a mindset that life is all about just hanging out we will find ourselves old with little to show for our time here on planet earth.

I once read a now out of print book (I don't have the details on title and author) where it shared the results of the study of five hundred top CEOs. The study covered how they handled their work and their personal life. The conclusion was that only 4 per cent were top performing in both areas. Those twenty CEOs were at a high level able to consistently consider what was the best use of their time from moment to moment during each day. They were able to know what activities to focus on at work and what to focus on in their personal life. As well they knew when personal needed greater focus than work and vice versa.

These CEOs had thriving businesses and thriving personal lives. These desirable results did not happen by simply going with the flow and doing what came naturally.

They considered their objectives and planned accordingly. They then followed through on those plans. They of course were also clear on what was important and what needed to be done to achieve success. This brings up the importance of planning one's life and ensuring it ends in the most desirable way.

Planning is a stretch for many people. It forces people to consider what is important to them and what it will require to achieve. This involves a type of thinking which most people are unaccustomed to. As well it doesn't have immediate payback. For example if a person is constantly in a state of busyness there is a certain payback from busyness. It feels like they are being productive because they are doing something. It may not be the best thing to do and it may not be done in the most effective or efficient manner but in the whirl of activity that is not even considered. After all he or she is busy. The itch is being scratched. The activity of planning can seem like a waste of time because it involves thinking rather than doing. As well many people have become jaded about the process of planning due to "fake" planning. This is when plans are cranked out to satisfy upper management but little true thought is put into them and they are never seriously considered in the day to day operations.

We have an example of where the importance of planning is illustrated in Evansing. I have repeated a portion of what I previously shared in Chapter 11:

"Great! Thanks, Percival. Now for my plan, mind you I haven't really thought about it in any great detail. I haven't thought about it in any detail other than this: You turn into a big bird, I jump on your back, we fly to Grange and we take out the bad guy.'

'That's about how detailed I thought your plan would be. Hmm, I think we need to consider some additional thoughts on the matter. One matter is how we approach Grange without being detected. Brydon is sure to have ways of picking up any movements towards him.'

'Why don't we go under the cover of darkness?'

Percival responded, 'Brydon sees as clearly
in the darkness as we see in the noon day
sun. No, we will have to consider other factors
besides darkness as a potential covering.'

'What about the altitude we fly at? Do you
know if his power gets weaker if we go
higher than normal?' asked Edwin.

'Good question. Let me ponder it and see
what comes to me. Another matter is how
are we going to enter the castle? Do we
enter on foot or fly over the castle walls?
Both have pros and cons. That is something
else I will ponder."

# Personal Power

*Chapter Twenty Six*

First read the following from Evansing:

"True kings know they are given positions of power and influence to benefit people, not simply to enjoy advantageous situations for themselves."

Much has been written about personal power. It is important to have personal power in order to achieve our goals in life. The above excerpt from Evansing makes it clear that power is also meant to benefit others, not only ourselves. In a perfect world everyone would be looking for opportunities to exercise their power for the well-being of others. Since we do not live in a perfect world it is up to us who have awareness of our responsibility to exercise power to help others.

Power is defined by Google as following:

The ability to do something or act in a particular way, especially as a faculty or quality.

The capacity or ability to direct or influence the behavior of others or the course of events.

In order for Power to be exercised there must awareness that we do in fact have it. I would say a great number of people don't even think about their personal power. This is because many people have been so disempowered by life experiences that the idea of being able to influence their world is quite foreign to them. It is a vital truth all persons need to grasp at a deep level. Without that deep revelation a person will forever feel they are at the mercy of whatever life throws at them. This results in great frustration and a sense of help-lessness. Getting that revelation can be a deeply moving experience. This is because it contradicts deeply rooted beliefs working counter to one knowing they have power. Edwin got a revelation from Greer he could mull over to reinforce his level of power as noted below:

"Like everyone else in the party of thirty or so representatives from Evansing he was excited to go to Nerland. He also struggled with self-doubts about his ability to impact the Nerland military. Then he remembered what Greer had said about him being a mighty prince. He mulled it over and over until after a while the self-doubts had gone and indeed he felt like a mighty prince."

Awareness of one's power is a tremendous boost to a person's confidence to deal with whatever life brings. That confidence trans-lates into success being accomplished and further confidence being gained in the process.

Power can entail simply being able to love another person. To get there might take some effort and willingness to face discomfort. See the following from Evansing:

"Well first of all we need to continue working out some of your heart issues. For if you do not have a heart capable of loving a woman or another human, then rules will only be a source of frustration.'

For the next three hours the men started to do a deeper work with some of those hurts of abandonment and abuse. When they were done, Edwin felt like a limp rag. He had just relived and processed some major pain and had shed many tears. He felt sheepish for this non Irish warrior behavior. Percival, unfazed by all the tears joked that he still respected Edwin."

The above process created a new capacity in Edwin to at least love Greer at a higher level. A similar process can be used and even must be used to heal those lies created about being helpless and unable. We were all created to be powerful.

# Teachableness

*Chapter Twenty Seven*

Teachableness is not something you hear too much about in your typical success book. A major reason is it doesn't feed the ego. It requires humility. It probably incorporates all the other qualities at one time or another in order to successfully develop it and exercise it. Quite often it occurs after a significant setback where our judgment or actions are called into question. Even in far less significant situations it can be difficult to acknowledge we were wrong and have something to learn.

Being coachable is another way to say being teachable. Persons have to be teachable to receive the full benefit of being coached. They have to be willing to acknowledge they don't have all the answers and they need outside help with some important area or areas of their life.

Professional coaches won't even take on a prospective client if their initial interview indicates a lack of coachability. To attempt to coach someone who is not coachable is a frustrating exercise destined to fail. Best to leave them on the hot griddle of life until they are a little more done and have become more aware and amenable to being teachable. Of course there are some who will never be teachable. It is a sad but a true reality. Many people convince themselves they have nothing to learn from others. Hopefully before they get too burned they will gain the needed awareness. There may not always be obvious negatives resulting. Often it is just having a life somewhat less than what could have been available.

Humans have an innate hatred for being wrong or somehow not having it all together. This may come across as being pride and perhaps it is a type of pride.

Whatever it is, it interferes with personal growth. Humility is the opposite. It recognizes we are a work in progress and until the day we die there will always be something we can improve in. Humble people, those who have a low or modest view of themselves look at their "teachers" as gifts. Those teachers may be a nagging spouse, a disrespectful child, a tyrant boss or even someone who cuts them off in traffic. In each of these cases an opportunity to learn and grow is being presented. If we simply look at them as irritations, injustices or some other unfortunate part of our lives then we have missed the point. All these are instances of life wanting to make us more aware of who we are and how we could continue to do better. Cultivation of gratitude for these lessons will go a long way to create a productive response and reduce or eliminate needless friction in relationships.

Edwin showed a humble teachable attitude in his relating to Percival. He demonstrated his willingness to do whatever Percival required of him. This included doing things that would have at one time been abhorrent to his sense of what an Irish warrior would do. His goal of being a great husband and a great leader kept him focused on those end objectives and not on the painful process.

One attitude which greatly facilitates teach-ableness is the desire to learn and grow. When we are learning we are by definition attaining knowledge or insight about something we didn't have before. When we are in this mode we have decided we value the benefits of learning more than we value the comfort of not learning. We often are stifled in our pursuit of something because there is a discomfort we don't want to experience. Star athletes are on the other side of the spectrum. They embrace dis-comfort in their training and preparation for they know their coach wants them to win. Therefore when he tells them what they need to do, they do it. I heard once on a CD from a former officer in the Navy Seals that the members of that elite unit actually complained if the training was too easy.

Therefore when we are being trained hard it is important for us to recognize the deeper capacity being formed so we can perform at the level of excellence required.

This raises the matter of excellence. We must have an attitude of excellence. This is defined as the quality of being outstanding or extremely good. Some synonyms are superiority, brilliance, pre-eminence and greatness. These characteristics come at a cost. Often they require teachableness. As we align our thinking and feelings with the desirability of excellence over comfort it em-powers us to run roughshod over all those otherwise discomfiting obstacles. It is like a football player who is charging the line. He enjoys the challenge and does not focus on the difficulty or the pain of being hit by the opposition.

# Warrior

*Chapter Twenty Eight*

The word warrior radiates dynamism, action and risk. A warrior is someone on a mission he or she is willing to die for. In everyday life apart from war, most warriors are not expecting to or wanting to die in achieving their mission. They are often men and women in business who are engaged in a continual battle with competition and all the other obstacles hindering their attainment of what they have determined is important. Other warriors are battling what they consider as injustices. In some countries they become involved in real life or death struggles and bear arms to enforce their demands. In most countries they are using legal and peaceful means to achieve just ends.

In the following excerpt from Evansing we find an example of what it means to be and think like a warrior:

"Edwin chose to ride up front with the chief scouts to keep an eye out for anything suspicious. A half mile or so down the road Edwin noticed an unusual sight. Crows were sitting in the trees about a hundred yards on either side of where their entourage was going, but none appeared to be sitting in the area directly ahead near the road. He mentioned this to the chief scout who dismissed it as being the way it was sometimes. To him no possibility existed of there being a serious threat along this path. Edwin, however, had the advantage of not being lulled by the familiar. He knew for crows to do that must mean something or someone waited ahead. His experience as a hunter as well as a warrior had sharpened his senses to the unnatural. He mentioned his concerns again to the chief scout and said he felt it important to stop the procession and check out what lay ahead. The chief scout, sensing the urgency and also considering the respect

Edwin held as a warrior, decided he would do as advised. He and Edwin and the other scouts rode back to the party some seventy-five yards behind them and advised the King they had some concerns. They felt they should be investigated before continuing further. The King rather impatient to get going was tempted to dismiss it as being too cautious. However, he had high regard for Edwin's judgment so he agreed to stop the journey and have fifty or so troops go on and check it out."

We see how Edwin's experience as a warrior and as a hunter heightened his ability to notice the unusual. This ability saved lives and probably saved the life of King Erith. Without him the whole Evansing mission to unite Ireland into one kingdom would have come to a halt.

Some men see themselves as noble warriors in a battle to protect and support women and children. Others see themselves as warriors when playing sports or when engaging the world of business. A warrior perspective stimulates a battling heart-set which energizes a person to another level of determination of achievement and success.

Visualizing the outcome you want to create can help to create that warrior determination and confidence.

# Appendix

Congratulations! You have now completed reading a book designed to give you insight into how your life can be changed for the better. Specific steps have been given as to how to achieve that change.

The process of change is never easy. It requires thinking differently and doing things we have never done before, or at least doing them in a new way. There will be frustrations in trying to implement what we know we need to do. The old ways will keep creeping in and distracting you from the best. This will come from what appears to be important in the moment. Constantly you will need to check in with yourself as to what is the best thing to be done and the best way to do those things. If you stay the course you will progressively realize new gains in your life. This can be used to motivate you for continued application of what you know to be the right way to live your life.

A useful exercise would be to go back through the book and noting on a piece of paper all the action steps and ideas that strike you as something tangible you can start doing now. It is important to have a now mindset about what is possible for you. Start expecting every day something new and progressive.

You have freedom to make choices even when it doesn't seem like it. Yes, certain choices you would like to make may presently be out of your immediate power to attain. However here are some choices you can now determine to consistently choose: joy over sadness, peace over worry, courage over fear and kindness over unkindness. Our mind and emotions will tell us we have no power over these. This is a lie. Healing is available for those who seek to empower these choices. These base line choices made on a consistent basis will result in more and more of the other choices becoming available and attainable. They attract new ways of thinking and doing. They attract the right people and opportunities into your life. Stay the course and expect the change you want to start appearing as your normal life experience.

# About the Author

The author, Glen Klassen, had the idea of becoming an author after waking up one morning with the following words popping into his head: "The door inched open ever so gingerly." He went to his computer and wrote about the antics of gorillas that had escaped from the Cincinnati Zoo. After this initial short story he continued to write short pieces until the inspiration came for "Evansing – Heart of the Irish Kingdom" and from it "Unlimited – Anything is Possible."

Glen has a passion for growing in personal wholeness. He has invested much time and effort in the process of being restored. Consequently it is a subject in which he has gained substantial insight. He enjoys sharing

This knowledge and encouraging others to keep expecting anything is possible regardless of current circumstances.

The author is a professional accountant whilst also pursuing his passion of being an author. He considers the role of mentoring his four grandchildren to be one of his most important roles in life.

# Another book by
## Glen E. Klassen

"Evansing – Heart of the Irish Kingdom"

Eleventh century quest for Irish unity that moves a young man from meager beginnings to Crown Prince. The quest requires the hero's personal transformation as he collaborates with the supernormal in war and diplomacy. The tale involves extraordinary interventions to facilitate assassinations, rescues, winning battles and successful diplomacy. There is also romance as the hero marries the King's daughter.

This adventure is primarily driven by four main characters with the hero Edwin, playing the leading role. The plot is the process of bringing together the numerous small Irish kingdoms into one united Ireland. There is extensive dialogue filled with inspirational life wisdom about leadership, relationships and personal wholeness.

"Evansing – Heart of the Irish Kingdom" can be ordered at www.gleneklassen.com.

Made in the USA
San Bernardino, CA
11 February 2016